"Essential reading for those concern
fessionally with mental health—one
century. In *Politics of the Mind* Iaiı
account of why and how capitalism
distress we are experiencing. Lucidly
past and current sources, this book spans analysis and ways of collectively challenging the situation we find ourselves in."
—Ann Davis, Emeritus Professor of Social Work and Mental
    Health, University of Birmingham

"This book is a welcome return to a Marxist view of mental health
debates. Ferguson writes clearly about a complex topic and he invites
the reader to consider an important social materialist perspective,
which avoids the pitfalls of both biomedical and postmodern assumptions. An excellent read!"
—David Pilgrim, Professor of Health and Social Policy, University
    of Liverpool

"Iain's book is an unique contribution to understanding mental distress.
We live in a mad world where it's hard to remain sane. Iain takes us
through the story and why we don't have to live this way. I recommend
this book to all mental health workers.
—Salena Williams, senior nurse at liaison psychiatry Bristol Royal
    Infirmary and Unison international officer

"With this short text Iain Ferguson has provided us with a resource of
hope, so badly needed given the current crisis in mental health that is
set out clearly at the beginning of the book. This hope comes in large
part from the challenges being made to the dominant biomedical
model of mental ill-health, not only by the service user movement and
those critical psychiatrists and psychologists whom the author rightly
credits, but by the group of radical social workers that includes Iain at
its centre. Teeming with insights into the crucial interaction between
individual and social experience, this book will play a part in supporting the collective struggles required for more and better mental health
services, and for a better world."
—Guy Shennan, Chair, British Association of Social Workers,
    2014-2018

"A hugely impressive achievement. Compact and accessible, Ferguson's book is particularly strong on the debates around psychoanalysis and anti-psychiatry. His clear but nuanced perspective includes a strong sense of solidarity with those working or living with mental distress. A powerful indictment of a maddening society as well as a timely and urgent contribution to the fight for a better world."
—**Roddy Slorach, author of** *A Very Capitalist Condition: A History and Politics of Disability*

"The society we live in is producing an epidemic of mental ill health and this is making mental distress into a major social and political issue. The issue is both one of resources, continually under attack from neo-liberal governments, and one of analysis—how we understand and respond to distress. Iain Ferguson's excellent study navigates these complex questions with skill, humanity and, crucially, socialist politics: a book for our times."
—**John Molyneux, socialist writer and activist and editor of** *Irish Marxist Review*

**About the author**

Iain Ferguson is Honorary Professor of Social Work and Social Policy at the University of the West of Scotland. He is the author of several books, including *Global Social Work in a Political Context: Radical Perspectives* (with Michael Lavalette and Vasilios Ioakimidis, Policy Press, 2018). He is advisory editor of the journal *Critical and Radical Social Work* and is a member of the editorial board of *International Socialism*.

# Politics of the Mind

## Marxism and Mental Distress

### With a new updated introduction

Iain Ferguson

Bookmarks Publications

*Politics of the Mind: Marxism and Mental Distress*
Iain Ferguson

This edition published 2023
First edition published 2017
Bookmarks Publications
c/o 1 Bloomsbury Street, London WC1B 3QE
© Bookmarks Publications

Typeset by Peter Robinson and Simon Assaf
Cover design by Ben Windsor
Printed by Halstan Limited

ISBN 978-1-914143-69-4 (pbk)

# Contents

# Foreword

THIS short book has been a long time in the making. I first read R D Laing's *The Politics of Experience* as an 18-year-old in the early 1970s and, like many others of my generation, was blown away by Laing's central argument that madness could be "intelligible", had a meaning which was somehow related both to the way some families operated and also to the wider operation of capitalist society. For all their theoretical and political shortcomings, some of which will be discussed later in this book, Laing's writings were one important factor in leading me and many others of the "68 generation" to begin to question capitalism and the ways in which it shaped family life and mental health. The recent biopic of his life, *Mad to Be Normal*, starring David Tennant as Laing, is likely to rekindle debate and discussion around his ideas.

Since then, several other factors have also been important in deepening my interest in, and understanding of, mental health issues. While employed as a social worker in a psychiatric hospital in the late 1980s, I was fortunate to work over a two-year period with a support group for family members of people given a diagnosis of schizophrenia. The experience highlighted the practical and emotional challenges of caring for a son, daughter or sibling suffering from a severe psychotic condition and these families" own need for support. The current crisis in mental health provision, discussed in the opening chapters of this book, means that in reality such families are now left with even less support than they had then. Whatever ideological differences and debates there may be regarding the nature of mental distress, building unity in action between campaigning organisations of service users on the one hand and carers" organisations on the other remains an important political task if further cuts to services are to be prevented.

Later, as a social work academic, I was involved in undertaking qualitative interview-based research over ten years with different groups of people experiencing mental health problems including asylum seekers, people given the label of personality disorder and service users who were actively involved in managing services or playing a leading role in campaigning organisations. What was most fascinating about these conversations is that the issue of diagnosis rarely came up. Instead, people talked about their lives, the experiences (good and bad) that they had and the ways in which they understood and coped with their mental distress. I feel privileged to have been part of these conversations and learned a huge amount from them.

My own experience of anxiety and depression in my early thirties, triggered by stress and political burnout, forced me to address some previously unquestioned assumptions shaping my life and activities. The experience was a painful one and not one I would be in a hurry to repeat, but it was a valuable one nevertheless and one from which I learned a great deal.

Lastly, as a political activist, I have been involved over the years in many different campaigns around mental health as a socialist, a trade unionist and a member of the Social Work Action Network. Most recently these have usually been around the defence of services against cuts or even closure. What has been most inspiring about these campaigns, even when not successful, is the degree of unity they have succeeding in achieving between service users, trade unionists, professionals and campaigning organisations.

This book has benefitted from many discussions with colleagues, students, friends and comrades over the years. One person deserving of special thanks is my partner of 40 years, Dorte Pape, not only for her love and support but also for her knowledge and insights into the nature of mental distress as an experienced mental health social worker and also leader for many years of a highly innovative and empowering mental health homeless team. Her contribution to this book is considerable, based on many late-night discussions and her understanding of the social model of mental health in practice.

In addition I am grateful to Danny Antebi, Andy Brammer, John Molyneux, Rich Moth, Roddy Slorach, Jeremy Weinstein and Salena Williams for their comments on an earlier draft and to Sally Campbell and Lina Nicolli for their comments on chapter one. All these comments and suggestions were extremely helpful, even if I haven't always acted on them. Thanks also to Peter Robinson, Carol Williams, Simon Assaf and

Sandra Shepherd for their work on the production. Given, however, the highly contested nature of mental distress and the likelihood that almost everyone (especially my friends on the left!) will disagree with at least some of the arguments presented here, it is perhaps particularly necessary to stress that I alone am responsible for the book's contents.

Finally, I dedicate this book to our two children, Brian and Kerry, who despite their parents" undoubted shortcomings and the contradictions of the nuclear family under capitalism, have somehow nevertheless developed into warm, sociable and sensitive adults!

## A note on terminology

No critical exploration of mental health can avoid the issue of terminology. The language we use to describe our emotional and psychological experiences inevitably points to an underlying theory about the nature and origins of that experience.

Some Marxists, such as Peter Sedgwick, opted to use the language of "mental illness", not least to emphasise the often very disabling nature of some mental conditions, especially psychotic conditions such as those labelled schizophrenia or bipolar (what used to be called manic depression). More recently, some sections of the mental health user movement have sought to reclaim the term "mad", analogous to the gay movement's appropriation of terms like queer and dyke. However, as the editors of a recent collection of writings which looks at the application of the social model of disability to mental health issues have noted:

> [W]hile the term "madness" is often used as a shorthand for distress, mental illness or disorder, we are aware that some individuals reject the term as pejorative or stigmatising (Beresford et al, 2010). The word "distress" is often used by many users/survivors, but it is potentially too broad a term on its own to encompass the situation of people with very acute and long-term mental health difficulties, and it is these people who are more likely to be considered "disabled". In addition, we recognise that not everyone who is considered "mentally ill" experiences distress (although other people may be distressed by their situation or behaviour).[1]

In truth, there is no single term that fits everyone's experience. In this book, for reasons that will become clear in Chapter 2 where I address the limitations of the medical model, I will not be using the term "mental illness" Instead, for the most part I will use (relatively) neutral terms such as "mental distress" or "mental health problems" which I hope will be acceptable to most people, while recognising that even these terms do not always do justice to the depth and variety of the experiences and behaviours under discussion.

# Introduction to the 2023 edition

Much has happened since this book first appeared in print in late 2017. In this new introduction, I will focus on three developments since then that have relevance to the themes the book explores. These are first, the appearance of new or accelerating political and economic crises that have serious implications for people's mental health but beyond that, for life itself and the future of life on the planet; second, new challenges to the dominant biomedical ideology of mental distress; third, a political landscape that is in key respects very different from 2017.

## The Multiple Crises

First, there are the multiple crises—political, economic, ecological— that have emerged or deepened since 2017. Late 2019 saw the outbreak of a global Covid-19 pandemic that at the time of writing has taken the lives of more than 17 million people worldwide and continues to cause death, illness and misery around the globe. The environmental crisis, the product of capitalism's addiction to fossil fuels, has now worsened to the point where it threatens the very basis of life on the planet. A "cost of living" crisis beginning in 2022 has seen millions of people in the West forced to choose between feeding their families and heating their homes. And Vladimir Putin's decision to send Russian troops into Ukraine in 2022 following years of NATO expansion into Eastern Europe has led to an inter-imperialist conflict in Ukraine that risks spilling over into nuclear war. While each of these crises has its own specific features and dynamics, we make a mistake if we see them as unrelated. Rather, as Alex Callinicos has argued in his important new book *The New Age of Catastrophe*, their shared roots lie in a capitalist mode of production conceptualised by Marx as

> an economic system whose relations of production are constituted by two interrelated antagonisms: the exploitation of wage labour by capital and the competition between rival capitals (whether firms or states). These antagonisms give rise to a blind and unending process of competitive accumulation that...drives simultaneously environmental destruction, the Long Depression and the growing geopolitical rivalries.[1]

Here, I will focus on the first two of these crises—the Covid-19 pandemic and the environmental crisis—since there is more evidence for their impact on mental health than for the other more recent crises.

## Capitalism, Covid-19 and Mental Distress

In his discussion of the economic impact of the pandemic, historian Adam Tooze notes that "in the historic record of modern capitalism, there has never been a moment in which close to 95 percent of the world's economies suffered a simultaneous contraction in per capita GDP, as they did in the first half of 2020". But as he argues, simply focusing on the economics of the crisis fails to capture the pandemic's profound impact on people's health and well-being:

> It was, as we all experienced, a disruption that went far beyond anything that can be captured in statistics of gross domestic product (GDP), trade and unemployment. Most people had never suffered such a serious interruption to their everyday life. It caused stress, depression and mental anguish. By the end of 2020, the largest part of scientific research on Covid-19 was dedicated to mental health.[2]

In the early stages of the pandemic, bodies such as the Royal College of Psychiatrists in the UK predicted a "tsunami of mental illness" with its president, Adrian James, suggesting that Covid-19 posed "the greatest threat to mental health since the Second World War".[3] Figures from influential bodies such as the Centers for Disease Control and Prevention in the United States (CDC) and the World Health Organisation (WHO) seemed to confirm these grim predictions. The conclusion of a Scientific Brief published by the WHO in March 2022, for example, was that the pandemic, lockdowns and associated public health measures had led to a worldwide increase in mental health problems, including widespread depression and anxiety.[4]

More recent research has questioned some of these predictions. A widely reported systemic review of 137 studies from around the world led by researchers at McGill University in Canada and published in the *British Medical Journal* in March 2023 concluded that the pandemic had resulted in "minimal" changes in mental health symptoms among the general population.[5] Its publication was greeted with headlines such as "Mental-health crisis from Covid pandemic was minimal".

One explanation for these different assessments is that the impact of Covid on different sections of society has been very uneven, meaning that generalised studies such as the McGill study can be highly misleading.[6] At one extreme, the super-rich were able to sit out the pandemic on their private islands or yachts while at the same time massively increasing their wealth. According to an Oxfam report in 2022, the world's ten richest men more than doubled their fortunes from $700 billion to $1.5 trillion—at a rate of $15,000 per second or $1.3 billion a day—during the first two years of a pandemic that saw the incomes of 99 percent of humanity fall and over 160 million more people forced into poverty.[7]

For some sections of workers too, especially those who kept their incomes, the experience of lockdown had some beneficial aspects. It meant they were able to avoid the long commute to work, have less contact with bullying bosses and spend more time with their families (or in the garden)—one reason why so many workers were reluctant to go back to their workplaces after lockdown was lifted.

Then there is the collective nature of the pandemic. A large-scale study led by a team of experts from several British universities that measured levels of mental distress from the beginning of the pandemic found that levels of anxiety and depression were indeed much higher than during the first lockdown, particularly amongst people who had already suffered from mental health difficulties, who were poor, young or who had small children at home. However, following that initial phase the research team found that there was a reduction in levels of distress. According to lead researcher Richard Bentall:

> This picture of adaptation and resilience should not be surprising because we know from previous research that individual, interpersonal

traumas (for example, sexual assaults) are far more mentally damaging than collective traumas such as natural disasters. This is at least in part because strong social bonds protect people against stress and, during a crisis, people often come together to help each other, creating a sense of belonging and a shared identity with neighbours.[8]

I have argued elsewhere that some early research in the UK showed that a desire to protect the NHS meant that large numbers of people felt that they could tolerate long periods of lockdown without becoming too distressed—in other words, their beliefs and values were a protective factor for their mental health[9] (and arguably the lockdown in the UK was led from below, with a YouGov poll in March 2020 showing that 93 percent of people supported or strongly supported the first lockdown).[10]

Important as the large-scale studies mentioned above are, based on narrow diagnostic criteria they sometimes fail to do justice to the pain, grief and isolation that was the experience of millions of people across the globe during the pandemic. By 2023, more than 220,000 people had lost their lives due to Covid in the UK alone, with poor people and black and minority ethnic communities worst affected. Tens of thousands of elderly people died in care homes, including many who had been hurriedly moved there without testing in order to free up hospital beds. Families suffered the unimaginable pain and grief of being unable to be with their relatives as they died (a pain later made worse by revelations of partying within the Tory government while the mass of ordinary people adhered to social distancing rules). Hundreds of thousands of disabled people were left to cope on their own as care services were withdrawn. More than 2 million people have been left suffering with long Covid, with studies showing that one in four people with this condition experience mental health problems. Many health and social care workers have experienced "moral injury" as a result of not being able to give those they look after the quality of care they require; and while trade unions, including the National Education Union, were right to oppose the premature lifting of lockdown by a Tory government desperate to get back to "business as usual", there is no doubt that children in particular struggled with the social isolation and loss of schooling the lockdown produced. As Edinburgh University academic Devi Sridhar has argued, lockdown was the least worst option:

The truth is that they [lockdowns] were an extreme public health response and were only taken up as public policy because of the even worse option facing countries, of imminent (and real) healthcare collapse and mass death. No one is pro-lockdown; this was about being anti-mass death.[11]

In this connection, it cannot be stressed too often that the enormous toll of death and suffering attributable to the pandemic was not simply the inevitable outcome of a natural disaster. Rather, as the evolutionary biologist Rob Wallace and the late Mike Davis have argued, there was very little that was "natural" about the origins of this pandemic, the ways in which it spread or the degree of death and devastation that it wrought across the globe. All of these processes were shaped by factors such as global agribusiness's relentless expansion into forest habitats, the response (or lack of response) of national governments to the disease, decades of under-funding of public health systems and the impact on rates of infection and death of existing divisions and inequalities.[12]

## Climate Change and Mental Distress

The same holds true for the second major crisis facing humanity—climate change. While the direct and indirect effects of climate change on mental health have only recently been recognised, the available research evidence suggests that these too are considerable. So, for example, a 2021 review of the international literature by the Grantham Institute at Imperial College found a relationship between higher temperatures and the number of suicides. The Imperial study also found clear evidence for severe mental distress following extreme weather events such as floods; that people who already meet the criteria for mental illness are more vulnerable to the effects of climate change on both physical and mental health; and that climate change exacerbates mental distress, particularly among the young, even for individuals who have not been affected.[13]

Similarly, a 2023 survey by the British Association for Counselling and Psychotherapy (BACP) and YouGov found that almost three quarters (73 percent) of 16- to 24-year-olds reported that the climate crisis was having a negative effect on their mental health, compared with 61 percent of all people in the UK. The figures were up from 61 percent and 55 percent respectively in 2020.[14] One report on the study quoted the mother of a 14-year-old living in Britain who woke her up at midnight because she was worrying about the Willow Project, the oil and gas drilling scheme in Alaska that had recently approved by US president Joe Biden:

> I think for that generation, it's very scary—first the pandemic and then Putin invaded Ukraine and there was the whole nuclear threat. She was terrified about that... She is apathetic about studying because she doesn't see the point when the world is going to end anyway... She's worrying about things she can't control. She's really scared of the world she's going to be released into. It's hard, because her fears are founded in reality. It's not like the monsters-under-the-bed fears of small children. These are real concerns that I can't just magic away.[15]

Such distress is sometimes referred to as "climate anxiety" or "eco-anxiety". While these terms may be helpful for some people, as Gareth Morgan, co-chair of the Association of Clinical Psychologists" Climate Action Network has argued, they risk locating the problem within the person, "that they're too sensitive or are having irrational thoughts". Regarding climate anxiety as an individual problem implies that "not being concerned about the climate crisis is a healthy norm". By contrast, Morgan points to research showing that what does help is "participation, activism and connection with other people... When you are connected to other people, that distress, that feeling there is something wrong with you for feeling this way, dissipates because you feel you are making a difference".[16] Morgan's comments support the argument I make in the final chapter of this book that collective resistance is important to challenge both exploitation and oppression and also the feelings of powerlessness and isolation that a society based on alienation produces.

## Challenging the Medical Model of Mental Distress

The second new development I wish to discuss, while not of the same order of importance as the crises described above, is significant in terms of this book's central argument that the roots of the current mental health crisis lie primarily not in our brains or genes but in a system that fails to address our most basic emotional needs. Since 2017, considerable additional support for that argument has come in the form of new research (or comprehensive reviews of existing research) and research-based publications.[17]

Two contributions are particularly worthy of note. First, there is the work of Joanna Moncrieff, psychiatrist, author and founder of the Critical Psychiatry Network. On top of her earlier pioneering work challenging the dominant assumptions about how psychiatric drugs work (or don't work), more recent research led by Moncrieff has refuted the long-held view of depression as resulting from the lack of the chemical serotonin in the brain.[18] Moncrieff is also unusual in explicitly locating her understanding of the mental health system within a Marxist framework.[19]

Second, the Power Threat Meaning Framework (PTMF), written by a group of senior psychologists and service users and published in 2018 by the British Psychological Society (though not official BPS policy), is an ambitious and accessible attempt to develop alternative understandings of mental distress, a major development of the new paradigm discussed in chapter five of this book based on a detailed critical analysis of a huge range of research.[20] Running to over 400 pages on the free online version (a shorter introductory text is also available),[21] its aim, in the words of one of its authors, is to offer:

a new, non-medical perspective on why people sometimes struggle with a whole range of overwhelming emotions and experiences such as confusion, fear, despair, hopelessness, mood swings, hearing voices, self-harming, panic, eating difficulties, and so on. The PTMF argues that distress of all kinds, even the most severe, is understandable in the context of our relationships and social circumstances, and the wider structures, norms and expectations of the society and culture we live in.[22]

The Framework,

highlights the links between wider social factors such as poverty, discrimination and inequality, along with traumas such as abuse and violence, and the resulting emotional distress or troubled behaviour... The Framework describes the many different strategies people use, from automatic bodily reactions to deliberately-chosen ways of coping with overwhelming emotions, in order to survive and protect themselves and meet their core needs.[23]

Publications like the PTMF as well as trauma-informed literature such as Gabor Maté's *The Myth of Normal,* which locate the roots of current levels of mental distress in societal processes that deny our most basic social and emotional needs, provide important ammunition to challenge a biomedical model that locates that distress in faulty brains and genes. By themselves, however, even such well-evidenced critiques are unlikely to displace dominant ideology, policy and practice, for three reasons.

First, from a ruling-class perspective, there is obvious ideological value in promoting an approach that locates mental distress within individuals and characterises it as "illness" or "disorder", thus shifting attention away from the (well-documented) material origins of that distress in poverty, inequality and oppression.

Second, the unequal relationship between the pharmaceutical industry, the psychiatric profession and general practitioners means that biomedical understandings of mental distress and drug-based responses are built into the day-to-day practice of mental health services. The writer James Davies gives the example of two short questionnaires introduced into the NHS in the early 2000s designed to enable the average doctor to determine within five minutes if a person had depression (PHQ-9) or anxiety (GAD-7). A criticism of the questionnaires was that they both set the bar very low for forms of depression or anxiety for which a drug should be prescribed. So, for example, if you ticked the box to indicate that in the last two weeks you had suffered from poor appetite, troubled sleep and low energy and concentration "nearly every day", you would meet the category of "moderate depression", sufficient within NHS guidelines to be prescribed an anti-depressant. What most people could not know was that the questionnaires were designed, copyrighted and distributed throughout the NHS by Pfizer Pharmaceuticals who also happened to make two of the most prescribed anti-depressant and anti-anxiety drugs used in the UK. As Davies comments:

> So here we have a company setting the bar very low for receiving such drugs, while at the same time making and profiting from these drugs. And this has been going on unchecked in the NHS for many years.[24]

Third, for many years the demand from mental health service user organisations has been for "more and better" services—"better" meaning less coercive, less medicalised services with more equal relationships between users and workers and more scope for relationship-based talking therapies. There is no shortage of examples of what these approaches might look like, from the successful Open Dialogue model of work with people labelled "schizophrenic" in Finland to the international Hearing Voices Networks to user-led community-based cafés and social crisis centres. However, in the wake of the Covid pandemic, the ongoing crisis in the NHS and more than a decade of cuts and privatisation in mental health services, the reality is likely to be "fewer and worse" services in the future. A National Audit Office Survey of 33 of England's 54 specialist mental health trusts in 2023 found that, in response to severe pressure, "most" trusts had allowed waiting times and lists to increase; 15 had raised the threshold for how ill people had to be before they got care; and six had cut back the services they offered.[25] Research based on freedom of information requests published in April 2023 found that a quarter of a million children in England, including children who were self-harming or had attempted suicide, had been denied help because they did not meet the very high eligibility criteria for treatment.[26] And a report in March 2023 revealed that the UK government intended to halve the £500 million promised to invest in the staffing of the social care sector, despite there being more than 165,000 vacancies in the sector.[27] The consequences of that chronic shortage of health and social care services will be increased reliance on medication as a response to mental distress on the one hand and a much greater role for the police in responding to mental health emergencies on the other, leaving vulnerable adults in the care of forces that have often been found to be institutionally racist, sexist and homophobic.[28]

## The Return of Class Struggle

If well-argued critiques will not be sufficient to challenge the power of Big Pharma, let alone address the conditions that have given rise to the crisis in mental health, where then can we look for change? That brings us to the third development that has taken place since this book was written—namely, the very different political situation. In 2017, millions of people in Britain placed their hopes in the election of a Labour government under the leadership of veteran socialist Jeremy Corbyn to introduce progressive social policies that would challenge poverty and inequality. In Scotland, where the Labour Party's commitment to preserving the Union made it anathema to many, a 2014 referendum on independence generated a massive social movement with anti-austerity at its heart. Although unable to secure a majority for independence, the hope for change and the belief that "another Scotland was possible" saw membership of the Scottish National Party grow from 25,000 on the day of the referendum to over 125,000 three years later while the grassroots movement All Under One Banner could call huge demonstrations in support of independence across Scotland, including a demonstration of 200,000 people in Edinburgh in October 2019.

For reasons too complex to explore here, neither of these projects has proved politically capable of realising the hopes and dreams of their supporters.[29] As a result, in 2023 a weak and nasty Tory government under Rishi Sunak continues to clings to power through scapegoating Muslims, asylum seekers and trans people while facing no serious opposition from a Labour Party under Keir Starmer, which all too often responds to such scapegoating by attacking the Tories not from the left but from the right.

For all their political weaknesses, what both the Corbyn project in England and the independence project in Scotland offered was *hope*, the possibility of a different future. With the collapse of Corbynism and the fact that, at the very least, the prospect of Scottish independence is indefinitely postponed, there is a real danger that that hope can turn into cynicism and mass despair. That should concern us for three reasons.

First, as we have seen across Europe and in the United States, the combination of despair, scapegoating of minorities and the absence of a left alternative can fuel the rise of far-right and fascist parties. Such parties are a threat to all of us but perhaps most of all to oppressed minorities including people with disabilities or mental health problems, as I show in the discussion of psychiatry under the Nazis in Chapter 2.

Second, even without the horrors of Nazism, the election of far-right parties to government usually results in attacks on the gains brought about by the great social movements of the 1960s. Primarily this means attacks on ethnic minorities, women's rights and LGBT+ rights but it also affects understandings of mental distress, discussed in chapter four, that locate the roots of that distress in structural factors rather than alleged individual weaknesses. In Italy, for example, the far-right administration that covers the town of Trieste is pushing back many of the mental health reforms introduced there in the 1970s and 1980s under the supervision of the radical psychiatrist Franco Basaglia and promoting instead biomedical psychiatry and privatisation.[30] Similarly, social work academics in Brazil report that under the Jair Bolsonaro regime, there was growing pressure for "the return of psychiatric hospitals, outdated forms of pharmaceutical containment and total confinement".[31]

Thirdly, the hope offered by these movements did matter. At an individual level, hope is a key component in mental health recovery. One of the many criticisms of psychiatric diagnoses such as "schizophrenia" or "borderline personality disorder" is precisely that they remove hope and are experienced as life sentences. At a collective level, as I have argued elsewhere, social movements such as the Black Lives Matter movement which erupted following the murder of George Floyd by racist police in Minnesota in 2020 can play an important role in translating individual grief and powerlessness into collective solidarity and the hope of political change.[32] Conversely, the loss of hope can feed into depression and despair.

On a more positive note, since 2022 a new source of hope has appeared on the horizon: the return of class struggle beginning in June of that year with strikes by railway workers who were members of the RMT union. The period since has seen strikes by workers in other rail unions, Royal Mail workers, BT engineers, higher education staff, teachers in Scotland and England, civil servants, nurses, ambulance workers, junior doctors, workers in ports and oil rigs, workers in Amazon warehouses and many other local strikes including a long-running strike by coffin makers in Glasgow. The contrast with the preceding three decades can be summed up in one statistic: by January 2023, the total number of strike days for the preceding six months had hit 2.5 million, a figure last seen in 1989.[33]

The immediate reason for many of the strikes is a cost-of-living crisis that has seen huge rises in the cost of fuel bills and basic foodstuffs and that has left many low-paid workers forced to choose between heating their homes and feeding their families. But their roots go deeper. They follow two years of a pandemic during which working-class people made huge sacrifices and followed the rules in order to protect their own health and that of others. By contrast, as we now know, for those at the top of society it was "business as usual", with partying at 10 Downing Street and government ministers setting up a VIP lane to award lucrative contracts for Personal Protective Equipment (PPE) to their friends. These included the Scottish Tory peer Michelle Mone and her children, who secretly received £29 million originating from the profits of a PPE business that was awarded large government contracts after she recommended it to ministers.[34] So the strikes (which have had huge public support) are also an expression both of anger at the sheer hypocrisy of those who run society and of an unwillingness to make the further sacrifices they demand, especially following decades of neoliberal attacks on pay, conditions and public services.

In Chapter 1, I refer to a 2016 report on a conference on work-related stress which pointed to a correlation between the decline in the number of strike days in the UK since the 1990s and the rise in levels of mental distress with the writer suggesting there had been a shift "from picket lines to worry lines". The current rising level of strikes will not automatically lead to improvements in mental health. Apart from any other consideration, not all strikes win! And the experience since June 2022 has been of trade union leaderships restricting the strikes to a day here, a day there, and ending them as quickly as possible, often on the basis of a settlement well below the rate of inflation—effectively a pay cut. The fact that workers often lack the confidence to challenge these leaderships or to act independently is the result of decades of a low level of struggle (though at the time of writing, there are signs of that challenge beginning to happen in some unions, notably in higher education and among nurses).[35]

Nevertheless, with all their limitations, as the climate change example given above shows and as I argue in the conclusion to this book, the confidence and sense of collective agency that comes from fighting back can only be good for mental health. Marxists have always emphasised the importance of class struggle not only as a means of fighting exploitation and oppression but also because the experience of that struggle can lead workers to question the dominant ideas in society, whether it be ideas about asylum seekers undermining the NHS or about the role of the police being to protect us from crime. That twin role of struggle reaches its highest point in the course of socialist revolution. For Marx and Engels:

> Revolution is necessary not only because the ruling class cannot be overthrown in any other way, but also because the class overthrowing it can only in a revolution succeed in ridding itself of all the muck of ages and become fitted to found society anew.[36]

By "the muck of ages" Marx is referring to the ideas—for example, racism, sexism, nationalism—that the ruling class promotes to divide workers and to turn men against women, white against black, cis against trans and so on. But it also includes the ideas of inferiority, of lack of self-worth, of powerlessness that keep us passive and that can also fuel depression and other forms of mental distress, especially when the struggle is at a low level.

The German-Jewish Marxist Walter Benjamin described socialist revolution as "the brake" required to stop the train of capitalism plunging into the abyss.[37] That seems like a very distant possibility at present, in Britain at least. But the depth of the several crises discussed above means that "business as usual" becomes less and less of an option. As I write, just across the Channel, France is experiencing the biggest explosion of working-class anger since the heady days of May 1968, with millions of workers involved in demonstrations and strikes. The impact on workers' confidence and consciousness is well-expressed by Agathe, a striking rail worker, in an interview with *Socialist Worker*:

> We have forged links with employees from other sectors and that is very valuable in leading the fight. When we stop working, we take the time to think about the social and political organisation of the world, the wealth we create, and what society gives back to us, which is to say almost nothing. We think about the place that the leaders give us in this society and also about the place we would like to take. And that's why the strike is liberating.[38]

Whether or not that mass struggle will lead to a reconstruction of society depends on many factors, not least of which is the development of self-organisation among groups of workers and of socialist organisation at the heart of the struggle to combat the vacillations and sell-outs of the trade union leaders and the reformist politicians. But in a world where the physical and emotional health of the majority of people, even the very future of life on the planet, count for nothing against our rulers" relentless drive for profit, it is that struggle—the struggle of life against death—and the resistance of ordinary people across the globe that offers hope for the future.

# 1

# The crisis in mental health

## Introduction

Writing in the late 1950s, the radical American sociologist C Wright Mills drew a distinction between what he called "private troubles" and "public issues". Using the example of unemployment, he suggested that:

> When, in a city of 100,000, only one man is unemployed, that is his personal trouble, and for its relief we properly look to the character of the man, his skills, and his immediate opportunities. But when in a nation of 50 million employees, 15 million men are unemployed, that is an issue, and we may not hope to find its solution within the range of opportunities open to any one individual. The very structure of opportunities has collapsed. Both the correct statement of the problem and the range of possible solutions require us to consider the economic and political institutions of the society, and not merely the personal situation and character of a scatter of individuals.[2]

The crisis in mental health has become one of the key "public issues" of the 21st century. According to the World Health Organisation, depression now affects 350 million people worldwide and by 2020 will be the leading cause of disability in the world.[3] A 2014 study of data and statistics from community studies in European Union (EU) countries, Iceland, Norway and Switzerland found that 27 percent of the adult population aged 18 to 65 had experienced at least one of a series of mental disorders in the past year, including problems arising from substance use, psychoses, depression, anxiety and eating disorders, affecting an estimated 83 million people.[4] In the UK, one in four people will experience a mental health problem in any given year. Here, mental health problems are responsible for the biggest "burden" of disease—28 percent as opposed to 16 percent each for cancer and heart disease.[5]

That burden, however, is far from being evenly spread. As a 2017 report from the UK-based Mental Health Foundation showed, your chances of becoming mentally unwell are much greater if you are poor or low-paid:

> The most significant demographic differences relate to household income and economic activity. Nearly three quarters of people (73 percent) living in the lowest household income bracket (less than £1,200 pm) report that they have experienced a mental health problem in their lifetime compared to 59 percent in the highest (over £3,701 pm).[6]

And for people who are unemployed, the chances of becoming unwell are even higher:

> A very substantial majority of those currently unemployed (85 percent) report that they have experienced a mental health problem compared to 66 percent in paid employment (61 percent of people in full-time employment) and 53 percent of people who have retired.

One reason for that extraordinarily high figure may well be the massive pressure placed on unemployed and disabled people since the financial crash of 2008 to find work at any cost, a pressure reinforced by benefit cuts and loss of benefits through a brutal sanctions regime. In England referrals to mental health teams have risen by 20 percent at a time when mental health services have been cut by 8 percent. As one leading health policy academic has written:

> The links between financial problems and mental illness are quite well known to those working in the mental health field. Unemployment, a drop in income, unmanageable debt, housing problems and social deprivation can lead to lower well-being and resilience, more mental health needs and alcohol misuse, higher suicide rates, greater social isolation and worsened physical health. To give one example, 45 percent of people who are in debt have mental health problems, compared with only 14 percent of those who are not in debt. Moreover, the effects of a macroeconomic downturn affect the mental health not only of some adults but also of their children. Numerous studies have also shown the effect of general economic recession and unemployment on the rate of suicides and suicide ideation.[7]

In Greece, the brutal austerity policies imposed by EU institutions and the International Monetary Fund (IMF) since the financial crash of 2008 (and implemented since 2015 by the formerly left wing Syriza government) have been described by one leading player as "mental water-boarding". According to health economist David Stuckler, who has studied the impact of austerity policies on suicide rates across the globe, in terms of "economic" suicides "Greece has gone from one extreme to the other. It used to have one of Europe's lowest suicide rates; it has seen a more than 60 percent rise." In general, each suicide corresponds to around 10 suicide attempts and—it varies from country to country—between 100 and 1,000 new cases of depression. In Greece, says Stuckler, "that's reflected in surveys that show a doubling in cases of depression; in psychiatry services saying they're overwhelmed; in charity helplines reporting huge increases in calls".[8]

Attacks on benefits, cuts to health and social services and government and media campaigns to demonise unemployed and disabled people as "scroungers" and "shirkers" have all taken a toll on the mental health of people in these groups, as well as leading to an increase in hate crime. But the mental health of those in employment has also suffered as a result of the neoliberal policies of the past three decades. In 2015/2016 stress accounted for 37 percent of all work-related absences and 45 percent of all working days lost due to ill-health.[9] The intensification of work, which has been a key element of the neoliberal project, is one reason for this epidemic of work-related stress. So too, however, is the failure of trade union leaderships to organise effective resistance to neoliberal attacks, despite numerous opportunities to do so. As one journalist observed after sitting through a conference on the topic of work-related stress:

> The more I listened the more it seemed that the mental health of individuals had become the battleground in what might once have involved broader standoffs. (It was tempting to think that the frontline of labour disputes had shifted from picket lines to worry lines and that collective grievances had become individual psychological battles; in the 1980s an average of 7,213,000 working days were lost each year to strikes; that number fell to 647,000 between 2010 and 2015. Meanwhile the days lost to stress-related illness went exponentially in the other direction, including a 30 percent increase in occupational stress between 1990 and

1995.) Stress appears to be standing in for older concepts like injustice, inequality and frustration, seen at the level of the individual rather than of the wider workforce.[10]

In reality, few are unaffected by the relentless pressures of competition which have become even more intense in capitalism's neoliberal phase. The Mental Health Foundation report cited above found that only 13 percent of those surveyed described themselves as having "good mental health".

This is a problem for two major groups in society. On the one hand, it is a problem for the capitalist class. As Chris Harman observed: "The capitalist wants contented workers to exploit in the same way that a farmer wants contented cows".[11] Unhappy, stressed-out workers are less productive. Hence the growth in recent years of a global "happiness industry", often supported by national governments and big business, which monitors the "happiness" levels of the population and promotes individualised ways of dealing with stress (such as "positive psychology").[12] But neither these initiatives, nor repeated but empty government promises of more spending on mental health, go anywhere near addressing the roots of the problem.

The crisis in mental health is a much bigger problem, however, for the rest of us—for the 99 percent, the vast majority of the world's population who have nothing to sell but their labour power and many of whom are currently paying with their health, both mental and physical, for the failings of a system over which they have no control. And while one can admire the spirit of resistance reflected in service user movement slogans such as "Glad to be mad" and while much can sometimes be learned from the experience of mental distress, for most people the reality is sheer suffering. In a discussion of his own experience of depression for example, the journalist Tim Lott wrote:

> Depression is actually much more complex, nuanced and dark than unhappiness—more like an implosion of self. In a serious state of depression, you become a sort of half-living ghost. To give an idea of how distressing this is, I can only say that the trauma of losing my mother when I was 31—to suicide, sadly—was considerably less than what I had endured during the years prior to her death, when I was suffering from depression myself (I had recovered by the time of her death).[13]

Even R D Laing, the most prominent figure in the "anti-psychiatry" movement of the 1960s and 1970s, in his later writings protested that:

> I have never idealised mental suffering or romanticised despair, dissolution, torture or terror... I have never denied the existence of patterns of mind and conduct that are excruciating.[14]

The limitations of seeing mental distress as an illness will be discussed in the next chapter. For some, however, the strength of that term is that it is an *evaluative* concept—few people would choose to be ill. As the late Peter Sedgwick argued in a critique of Laing, Thomas Szasz and other anti-psychiatry thinkers of the 1960s and 1970s:

> Mental illness, like mental health, is a fundamentally *critical* concept; or can be made into one provided that those who use it are prepared to place demands and pressures on the existing organisation of society. In trying to remove and reduce the concept of mental illness, the revisionist theorists have made it that bit harder for a powerful campaign of reform in the mental health services to get off the ground.[15]

The arguments for and against Sedgwick's position will be considered in Chapter 4. Where he was undoubtedly correct, however, was in arguing that in the face of this vast ocean of emotional misery and pain, we cannot be neutral. A key aim of the Marxist approach outlined below therefore is not only to make sense of mental distress but also to help us address and change the material conditions that give rise to it.

### Capitalism and mental distress

Simply stated, the central argument of this book is that it is the economic and political system under which we live—capitalism—which is responsible for the enormously high levels of mental health problems which we see in the world today. The corollary of this argument is that in a different kind of society, a society not based on exploitation and oppression but on equality and democratic control—a socialist society—levels of mental distress would be far lower. A similar point was made more than 30 years ago by George Brown and Tirril Harris in their classic study of depression in women:

> While we see sadness, unhappiness and grief as inevitable in all societies we do not believe this is true of clinical depression.[16]

This is a strong claim which challenges the currently dominant orthodoxy regarding mental health problems. That orthodoxy sees anxiety and depression—and even more so conditions such as schizophrenia and bipolar disorder—as illnesses originating in the brain, identical in all key respects to physical illness, to which the most appropriate responses are medication or some form of physical intervention such as electro-convulsive therapy, sometimes coupled with psychological interventions. The limitations of what is usually referred to as "the medical model" will be explored more fully in Chapter 2. Before then, however, it is necessary to clarify the claim that the origins of many current mental health problems stem from the society in which we live.

Firstly, it does not mean that in a more equal society, there would be no unhappiness. Relationships would still break up, people would grieve the loss of loved ones, individuals would experience frustration and pain at not always being able to achieve their goals. Such experiences are part of the human condition. But as Brown and Harris suggest, there are good grounds for arguing that such painful experiences would be far less likely to develop into serious mental distress in a society without exploitation and oppression.

Secondly, to argue that mental health problems are the product of capitalism is not to suggest that such problems have not also existed in earlier types of society. The ways in which neoliberalism, the particular form of capitalism which has been dominant for over three decades, has shaped the mental health of millions of working class people, from the increased anxiety of schoolchildren due to never-ending tests to the loneliness and social isolation of many older people in an increasingly individualised society, will be addressed in a later chapter. Clearly, though, such problems did not begin with the election of Margaret Thatcher as UK prime minister in 1979 nor with Ronald Reagan as US president in 1980. Nor did it begin with the development of capitalism in the 14th century. Madness and mental distress, however defined, have been around for a long time. That said, as I shall show, both the extent of mental health problems in the world today as well as the particular forms which they take are to a very large extent the product of a society based not on human needs but on the drive to accumulate capital.

Thirdly, while everyone's mental health is damaged to a greater or lesser degree by the pressures of living in a capitalist society, clearly not everyone is affected in the same way. Mental health is shaped by the specifics of people's individual life experiences—good and bad—as well as by wider structural factors such as racism or sexism. That sense of the complexity of mental distress, especially psychosis or what is usually referred to as madness, is well-captured by Isaac Deutscher in his account of the exiled Trotsky's response to the news that his daughter Zina, who had been suffering from mental health problems for some time, had committed suicide in Berlin, just weeks before Hitler's accession to power:

> Distressed and shaken with pity, Trotsky was a prey to guilt and help-lessness. How much easier it was to see in what way the great ills of society should be fought against than to relieve the sufferings of an incurable daughter! How much easier to diagnose the turmoil in the collective mind of the German petty bourgeoisie than to penetrate into the pain-laden recesses of Zina's personality! How much superior was one's Marxian understanding of social psychology to one's grasp of the troubles of the individual psyche![17]

Any satisfactory Marxist understanding of mental health issues must therefore seek to do justice to the complexity of that interaction between individual and collective experience.

### A Marxist framework for understanding mental health

What then are the key components of a Marxist approach to understanding mental health? Three are particularly important and underpin the arguments in this book.

### A materialist approach[18]

A materialist approach starts from the recognition that human beings are biological animals with a range of needs which, if not met, will at best harm or stunt their development and at worst result in death. Thus, good health, both physical and mental, depends on the availability of such basic material preconditions as food, water, light and so on. Where these conditions do not exist, health suffers. As an example, a study published in 2017 found that people who lived near busy roads with high volumes of traffic had an increased risk of developing dementia.[19] Similarly, the incidence of schizophrenia varies significantly between industrial and rural societies, as do recovery rates.[20] How a materialist approach views the relationship between brain, mind and life events, as well as recent developments in neuroscience, will be discussed in Chapter 5.

But as well as the basic physical needs which humans share with other species there is also a range of social, emotional, psychological and sexual needs which are specific to humans. Marx's own views will be discussed more fully in Chapter 6, but in his study of Marx's view of human nature, Norman Geras argued that for Marx one need in particular went to the heart of what it means to be human, namely:

> The need of people for a breadth and diversity of pursuit and hence of personal development, as Marx himself expresses these, "all-round activity", "all-round development of individuals", "free development of individuals", "the means of cultivating [one's] gifts in all directions", and so on.

As Geras comments:

> Marx does not of course take it to be a need of survival, as for example nourishment is. But then, besides considering the survival needs common to all human existence, he is sensible also...of the requirements of "healthy" human beings, and of what is adequate for "liberated" ones; he speaks too of conditions that will allow a "normal" satisfaction of needs. These epithets plainly show that for all his well-known emphasis on the historical variability of human needs, he still conceives the variation as falling within some limits and not just the limits of bare subsistence. Even above subsistence level too meagre provision of, equally repression of, certain common needs will be the cause of one kind of degree of suffering or another: illness or disability, malnutrition, physical pain, relentless monotony and exhaustion, unhappiness, despair. This requirement, as Marx sees it, for variety of activity has to be understood in this sense, not as precondition for existence but as a fulfilled or satisfying, a joyful one.[21]

Our capacity for development, then, for what Aristotle calls "human flourishing", is at the core of what makes us human. As Terry

Eagleton argues, however, it is precisely this quality, which sets us apart from other species, which has been repressed for most of human history:

> Animals that are not capable of desire, complex labour and elaborate forms of communication tend to repeat themselves. Their lives are determined by natural cycles. They do not shape a narrative for themselves, which is what Marx knows as freedom. The irony in his view is that, though this self-determination is of the essence of humanity, the great majority of men and women throughout history have not been able to exercise it. They have not been permitted to be fully human. Instead, their lives have been determined for the most part by the dreary cycle of class society.[22]

Marx was not, of course, the only person to have had this insight. Freud similarly recognised that society (or "civilisation") was based on the repression of our most basic needs and desires, often leading to problems in mental health. For Freud, however, such repression was necessary and inevitable, the price we paid for living in society; for Marx by contrast, that denial of our most basic humanity was the consequence of a society—capitalism—based not on human need but on the drive to accumulate profit. In Chapter 6, we shall discuss the ways in which such alienation affects our mental health, an issue seldom addressed within the mental health literature.

### A historical approach

The second element of a Marxist understanding of mental health is that it involves a historical approach, in two senses. Firstly, it means recognising that both our understandings of mental health problems and also the forms that they take at any particular time are shaped by the social and economic relations of the wider society. So, for example, hysteria, a condition which was one of the most common mental health problems in the late 19th and early 20th centuries, is rarely encountered today. By contrast, anxiety, which was hardly recognised as a mental health condition 50 years ago, is perhaps the condition *par excellence* in the era of neoliberal capitalism.

A historical or biographical approach is also important, however, for understanding why particular individuals become mentally unwell. This is not to suggest an equivalence between structural causes and individual causes. As Emile Durkheim demonstrated in his classic study of suicide in the 19th century, even the apparently most personal acts such as the decision to take one's own life are shaped by wider historical and sociological factors such as religion and geography.[23] Nevertheless, as the example of Zina quoted above shows, it is commonly the interaction of these wider historical processes (including in Zina's case witnessing the growth of the Nazis) and personal biographical factors (feeling abandoned by her father at a very early age, her enforced separation from her own children by Stalin) that results in mental health difficulties. In *Psychopolitics*, Peter Sedgwick rightly lamented the fact that students in the 1980s in professions such as social work and medicine were rarely taught how to take a full social history, something which Sedgwick saw as essential for a deeper understanding of the causes of an individual's mental distress. To quote two writers of a recent text on the causes of mental health problems (and to anticipate some of the arguments developed later in this book):

> If there is a key message, it is perhaps that we aren't born with the problems we have as adults, they aren't somehow inherently and inevitably built into our brains; they come from our interactions with other people, especially but not exclusively early on in life.[24]

The key point is that such interactions do not occur in a vacuum: they are structured by the dominant oppressions within society, principally around gender, race, sexual orientation and above all, class. Anxiety disorders, for example, occur more frequently among women than among men; levels of psychosis are higher in some BME communities than in white communities; and psychological problems (as well as rates of suicide and attempted suicide) are higher in the LGBT population.[25] And as we saw above, if you are poor, you are more likely to suffer from almost every form of mental health problem going. In addition, as Richard Wilkinson and Kate Pickett have shown in their best-selling book *The Spirit Level*, the more unequal the society you live in, the greater your chances of becoming mentally unwell.[26] That said, in understanding why particular individuals become unwell while others do not, it is often that interaction between structural factors and personal biography that is crucial.

## A dialectical approach

This emphasis on interaction points to the third component of a Marxist approach to mental health: namely, its dialectical character. As Rees argues:

> A dialectical approach is radically opposed to any form of reductionism because it presupposes the parts and the whole are not reducible to each other. The parts and the whole mutually condition, or mediate, each other. And a mediated totality cannot form part of a reductionist philosophy because, by definition, reductionism collapses one element into another without taking account of its specific characteristics.[27]

A dialectical approach to mental health therefore involves two elements. Firstly, a rejection of any form of determinism or reductionism. Most obviously, this refers to a biological reductionism which sees mental health problems as the product of chemical processes within the brain or the action of particular genes. It applies no less, however, to currently fashionable "early years" reductionism which sees the human brain as "fixed" from the age of three (or in some versions, three months); those psychoanalytic theories which reduce all behaviour to sexuality (or more frequently now, attachment issues); and mechanical Marxist approaches which fail to address the role of mediating factors, such as the family, in the production of mental health problems.

Secondly, a dialectical approach recognises that individuals and classes react back upon the circumstances that shape them, that "the parts and the whole mutually condition, or mediate, each other". A central argument of this book is that people's mental health is shaped above all by their life experiences under capitalism, usually mediated through work, family, school and the workplace. But the process is not simply one way. People *react* to their experiences, as opposed to simply being moulded by them. At an individual level they will seek to give meaning to them. And as Brown and Harris showed in the study referred to above, it is the *meaning* which people give to their experiences that is likely to determine whether or not they become depressed.[28] If, for example, a women who becomes unemployed blames herself and sees this as an example of her own worthlessness, in all likelihood she will develop a clinical depression; she is far less likely to do so, however, if she recognises that unemployment is a "normal" feature of life in a capitalist society.

But the meaning that people give to their experiences is not simply a product of their earlier life experience: it is also shaped by their *collective* experience of life under capitalism, not least the level of class struggle. As I will argue in Chapter 6, where working class people struggle against exploitation and oppression, it can have a profound effect on mental health, both individually and collectively. Where the level of class struggle is low, however, as it has been in the UK over the past few decades, then these injustices and the anger and frustration to which they give rise are much more likely to be internalised—hence, as noted above, the shift "from picket lines to worry lines".

## Structure of the book

Chapter 2 explores the ways in which ideas about madness and the experience of madness itself have developed through history and have been shaped by the class relations of the time. The main focus of the chapter will be on the emergence in the 19th century of what is now usually referred to as the medical (or biomedical) model of mental health. US President George W. Bush designated the 1990s as the "Decade of the Brain" and two decades later, approaches which locate the seat of mental distress in the brain and more generally see mental distress as an illness comparable in all important respects to physical illnesses, remain by far the dominant understanding and basis for treatment responses in most of the world. This chapter explores the strengths and weaknesses of this model, the reasons for its continuing dominance and the arguments against it, particularly those coming from critical psychologists and also from the service user movement which has developed in recent decades.

Until their displacement by biochemical and neurological approaches to mental health issues in the 1970s and 1980s, the dominant ideas within psychiatry through the middle part of the 20th century, especially in the USA, were based to a greater or lesser extent on the ideas of Sigmund Freud. Chapter 3 assesses the extent to which the human development theories of Freud and his successors are useful as a way of making sense both of the way in which personality is formed under capitalism and also of the roots of mental distress.

This is far from being a new enterprise. Generations of Marxists in the 1920s and 1930s, including leading Bolsheviks Leon Trotsky and

Karl Radek in Russia, the Frankfurt School and Wilhelm Reich in Germany, and the group of left psychoanalysts around Otto Fenichel, also in Germany, grappled with the ideas of Freud and the extent to which these were compatible with Marxism. Much of this history is relatively unknown and one aim of the chapter is to provide an account and assessment of these early debates.

For the most part, however, Freud's ideas and the practice of psychoanalysis have been deployed in a far from revolutionary way. Instead—and especially in the USA, where only medical doctors are allowed to practise as psychoanalysts—they have been incorporated into an essentially medical model (against the explicit wishes of Freud himself) and, like the biomedical approaches discussed above, used to individualise and depoliticise mental distress. A more political reading of Freud and a more critical psychoanalysis based on the ideas of Jacques Lacan emerged in France following the events of May 1968. The chapter will conclude with a brief discussion of these ideas and their relationship to Marxism.

The decade of the 1960s witnessed a great wave of social movements—the civil rights movement in the USA, the women's movement, the gay movement, the anti-Vietnam war movement—which challenged dominant ideas about the family, the role of women and also mental health and mental illness. Chapter 4 outlines and critically assesses the ideas of "anti-psychiatry" which emerged in several different countries in this period, focusing particularly on the work of the Scottish psychiatrist R D Laing.

The principal critic of Laing and of other leading figures in anti-psychiatry (Thomas Szasz, Erving Goffman and Michel Foucault) from the political left was Peter Sedgwick. The ideas of anti-psychiatry and Sedgwick's critique of them are of more than historical interest. Laing's life and work has been the subject of a 2017 movie while his ideas continue to resonate within sections of the mental health users' movement. Similarly, Sedgwick's seminal 1982 text *Psychopolitics* has recently been re-published and the book was the subject of a well-attended conference (and subsequent publication) at Liverpool Hope University in 2015, so a re-assessment of Sedgwick's arguments seems both timely and necessary.

The period since the start of the 21st century has seen the emergence of new radical currents in mental health. A coalition of critical psychiatrists and psychologists, radical social workers, activists and service users has contributed to the development of what has been called a "paradigm shift" in the understanding of mental health and mental distress. In place of a model which explains mental distress in terms of biochemical or genetic processes, the new paradigm, or world-view, locates "madness" and mental distress more generally primarily in people's life experiences. Chapter 5 outlines and assesses these new developments which seek to overcome some of the weaknesses and limitations of the earlier anti-psychiatry movement, while sharing many of its criticisms of the biomedical model. The chapter also addresses one of the most significant developments in mental health history, namely the emergence in recent decades of a social movement of mental health users and survivors committed to challenging the oppression experienced by people with mental health problems and to developing new forms of care and support.

The final chapter seeks to draw together the threads of the arguments from previous chapters into a rounded Marxist analysis of mental health and mental distress, central to which is the concept of alienation. A strength of some of the approaches to mental distress discussed in Chapter 5 is that, in contrast to biomedical models, they highlight the role of social and economic factors such as poverty, inequality and oppression in the creation of mental health problems. They often see such factors, however, as primarily the result of mistaken ideologies or misguided policies rather than being the necessary outcomes of a system based on competition and exploitation in which the vast majority of people have no control over what is produced or how it is produced. It is that lack of control that is the basis of Marx's theory of alienation and the first part of the chapter draws on that theory to explore the ways in which the lack of power and control which individuals experience as part of life under capitalism affects both their psyches and also their relations with other people.

The next part of the chapter explores the kind of services and policy responses we need to fight for in the here and now while recognising the danger that in a period of austerity some progressive approaches, such as the social model of mental health and recovery approaches, can all too easily become a cover for cuts in services in the name of promoting "independence".

The final part of the book looks ahead to a world driven not by the demands of profit but based on meeting human needs—material, social and emotional—and where for the first time, ordinary people will enjoy real power and control over their lives and can enjoy good mental health—a world which the Marxist psychoanalyst Erich Fromm called "the sane society".

# 2

# All in the brain?

In 2012, more than 50 million prescriptions for anti-depressants were issued in the UK, the highest number ever. In some parts of the country, such as the North West of England, one in six people are now prescribed anti-depressants in an average month.[29]

While the same period also saw an increase in the number of people being referred for psychological therapies (mainly cognitive-behaviour therapy), prescription of anti-depressants remains by far the most common response to someone presenting to their GP with the symptoms of depression.

Prescription on this scale is one indicator of the dominance of an ideology and approach (reinforced since 2010 in the UK by huge cuts to community-based alternatives) that sees depression, along with a wide spectrum of conditions ranging from anxiety to schizophrenia, as an illness requiring a medicalised response. That view, usually referred to as "the medical model", has shaped our understanding of health and mental distress since the 19th century. Harris and White define the medical model as stressing:

> the presence of an objectively identifiable disease or malfunction in the body, seen as a machine, with the patient regarded as the target for intervention by doctors using the latest drugs, technology and surgical procedures... In psychiatry, the approach is underpinned by a belief that the diagnosis of mental disorder is achieved by the accurate identification of an objective disease process.[30]

The first part of this chapter offers a short historical overview of ideas about "madness", including the development of the medical model. The following section considers some of the main critiques of that model, drawing on what is now a very extensive literature coming both from critical psychology and psychiatry and also from the service user movement. The final part of the chapter considers why, in the face of that critique, the medical model of mental health continues to shape dominant understandings of and responses to mental distress.

## Models of madness

Historically, explanations of what has traditionally been called "madness" have fallen into one of three camps: religious, medical and psychosocial. Unsurprisingly, for most of human history (and still today in much of the world) religious explanations have dominated. The Bible, for example, tells us that both Saul, the first king of the Israelites, and Nebuchadnezzar, the king of Babylon, offended god and as a punishment were both made mad. Within the *Illiad* and the *Odyssey*, the oldest surviving works of Western literature, as well as in the plays of the Greek dramatists Aeschylus, Sophocles and Euripides, there are many accounts of women and men becoming mad, most often at the behest of the gods. And as late as 18th century England, the idea that madness was caused by demonomania (possession by demons) was held by prominent public figures such as John Wesley, the founder of Methodism.[31]

Running alongside these religious views, and often in opposition to them, was a view of madness as located in the body or the brain, a view first put forward by the Greek physician Hippocrates of Kos (c460-357 BCE). Scull summarises the key elements of this model:

> [A]t Hippocratic medicine's core was the claim that the body was a system of inter-related elements that were in constant interaction with its environment. Moreover, the system was tightly linked together, so that local lesions could have generalised effects on the health of the whole. According to this theory, each of us is composed of four basic elements which contend for superiority: blood (which makes the body hot and wet); phlegm (which makes the body cold and wet, and is composed of colourless secretions such as sweat and tears); yellow bile or gastric juice (which makes the body hot and dry); and black bile (which makes the body cold and dry, and originates in the spleen, darkening the blood and stool). The varying proportions of these humours with which an individual is naturally endowed give rise to different temperaments: sanguine if generously supplied with blood; pale and

phlegmatic where phlegm predominates; choleric if possessed of too much bile.[32]

The balance between these humours could be affected both by internal factors (such as diet, lack of sleep or emotional turmoil) and by external factors (environmental conditions, war and so on), and one outcome could be disturbances of the mind. In that situation the role of the physician was to restore the balance between the humours through procedures such as blood-letting, purging and vomiting.

The model was a profoundly influential one. As Scull notes:

> Its central speculations about illness and its treatment would exercise an enormous influence, not just in Greece, but also in the Roman empire; and after a period when most such ideas were largely lost in Western Europe in the aftermath of the fall of Rome, they would be re-imported from the Arab world in the tenth and eleventh centuries. From then onwards, so-called humoral medicine would reign almost unchallenged as the standard naturalistic account of illness for many centuries, extending (albeit in somewhat modified form) into the early nineteenth century.[33]

The extent to which the use of physical treatments such as purging, blood-letting, vomiting and worse were still being employed in the treatment of the allegedly mentally ill in the late 18th century is vividly illustrated in Alan Bennett's play (and later film) about George III, *The Madness of King George*.

Humoral theories of mental distress can be seen as an advance on religious theories in that they purported to be based on a materialist/scientific, rather than a religious, approach and so challenged the stigma associated with madness by not viewing it as a form of divine punishment. That said, they were frequently opposed by, or co-existed with, such ideas, especially during periods of social upheaval including the rise of early capitalism. The period of the Reformation, for example, was accompanied by a massive witch hunt across Europe with between 50,000 and 100,000 women accused of being in league with the devil and possessed by demons being burned at the stake or perishing in equally gruesome ways at the hands of their religious persecutors.

Dominant ideas about madness and mental health, like the ruling ideas in general, are often challenged during periods of political and social change and upheaval. At such times the most progressive ideas do battle with the most reactionary ideas. The transition from feudalism to capitalism was one such period. And so the same society that saw women being burned at the stake as witches across Europe also saw, some 300 years before the birth of Freud and the creation of psychoanalysis, the emergence of humanistic ideas about madness which located its origins not in divine intervention or in humoral imbalances but in people's life experiences, particularly those of loss, pain, conflict and betrayal. As Scull observes, madness is a theme that runs through many of Shakespeare's plays, both the comedies and the tragedies. Titus Andronicus, for example, portrays "the madness of a world unhinged. It is a vision of moral codes dissolved, of humanity torn to shreds".[34] Meanwhile in King Lear, madness is naturalised:

> It emerges gradually as the King is buffeted by cold and by storms, but more importantly by the hammer blows of a series of overwhelming psychological onslaughts: betrayal by two of his daughters; the dawning realisation of his own foolishness and guilt; the death of Cordelia.[35]

As we shall see later, that same idea—that "madness" (psychosis) and milder forms of mental distress are rooted in our life experiences of loss or abuse—is also at the heart of current challenges to the medical model.

Ideas about madness were profoundly challenged again some two centuries later in another great period of political and social upheaval. Robert-Fleury's famous 1876 picture *Pinel Freeing the Insane* shows the mind-doctor Phillipe Pinel unchaining the female patients at the Salpêtrière hospital in Paris in the wake of the French Revolution of 1789 and extending to them the rights gained by the Revolution. As Fee and Brown suggest:

> The new "moral therapy" developed by Pinel and his contemporaries in the reformed asylums was fundamentally based on the idea of freeing mental patients' trapped humanity. This liberation allowed for a therapeutic doctor–patient alliance that was sensitive to the life situations and social circumstances of the "madmen" and "madwomen", who were formerly treated as subhuman.[36]

In England that same approach was represented in the "moral treatment" practised by William Tuke and his Quaker colleagues at the York

Retreat. Until that time only small numbers of those regarded as mad were locked up in hospitals. Instead, as Scull notes:

> As in centuries past, the primary burden fell upon families, and given the poverty and poor living conditions of the lower orders, the expedients employed were rough and ready. Chained in attics or cellars, or in outbuildings, the lot of these sufferers was still less enviable.[37]

The better-off mad, including most famously the Marquis de Sade, were often kept in the rapidly spreading private madhouses, the product of what Parry-Jones called "the trade in lunacy".[38]

The rise of moral treatment in the wake of the French Revolution, and the emergence of small asylums across the country, gave rise to hopes of a more humane approach to mental distress. Such hopes, however, were to be quickly dashed. As Pilgrim and Rogers comment:

> The realities of the pauper asylum system bore little relation to the aspirations of the reformers. Although some asylums tried to copy the moral treatment regime this was quickly abandoned as were all other therapeutic regimes. Like the workhouses, asylums quickly became large regimented institutions of last resort, which if anything were more stigmatising. Although they were run by medical men, they failed to deliver the cures that a medical approach to insanity had promised.[39]

An example of that degeneration is provided by the historian Barbara Taylor in her book *The Last Asylum*, which recounts her own experience of spending time as a patient in Friern Hospital in Middlesex shortly prior to its closure in the late 1980s. At its founding in 1851, Friern, or Colney Hatch as it was known then, was

> In conception at least, no gloomy Bedlam but a showcase for enlightened psychiatry. Its lovely grounds and elaborate frontage...signalled a prestige institution designed to comfort and heal the truant mind. Madhouses were notorious for "managing" their inmates with chains and whips, but now this new asylum, in quintessentially Victorian fashion, put them to work instead.[40]

Like other asylums, Colney Hatch became a self-supporting community with its own farm, orchards, bakeries and workshops. But as Taylor observes, like so many of these other asylums, created in every county by Act of Parliament, within a few decades Colney Hatch had become a byword for misery and degradation:

> In the second half of the nineteenth century asylum populations rose rapidly, as pauper lunatics crowded in from the workhouses and wards "silted up" with the "chronically crazy". Moral treatment foundered under the combined pressures of over-crowding, "cheeseparing economies, overworked medical superintendents, untrained under-supervised nursing staff". By the late 1860s most asylums had reintroduced strait-jacketing and other physical restraints. By the end of the nineteenth century the curative confidence of the asylum pioneers had vanished entirely to be replaced by a hereditary determinism as gloomy as the decaying buildings housing the "degenerates" and the "defectives" that the lunatics had now become. Care collapsed into custodialism, as the mad were pronounced "tainted persons" and the asylums became their prisons.[41]

Taylor's description of the experience of asylums such as Colney Hatch raises more general issues about the relationship between capitalism and mental health. Firstly, it shows the way in which progressive ideas and practices—in this case, more humane treatment of those with mental health problems—are subverted, undermined and distorted by the pressures and priorities of capitalist society (while acknowledging that moral treatment was also a form of social control).[42] Central to this was the issue of overcrowding. In 1827 the average asylum in Britain housed 116 patients; by 1910 the number was 1,072.[43] That growth continued through the 19th and 20th centuries so that even as late as the 1950s on an average day there were around 150,000 patients locked up in psychiatric hospitals in England and Wales. The reasons for that massive expansion are a matter of debate but three are particularly significant.

Firstly, there was the determination of the rising capitalist class (and not only in Britain) to separate out and segregate those who were able to work from those who could not. The "institutional solution", whether in the form of the workhouse, the prison or the asylum, was central to this. As Scull argued in an earlier work, *Museums of Madness*:

> The quasi-military authority structure which it [the asylum] could institute seemed ideally suited to the means of establishing "proper"

work habits among those elements of the work force who were apparently more resistant to the monotony, regularity and routine of industrialised labour.[44]

Secondly, there was the impact of industrialisation and urbanisation on the physical and mental health of individuals and families. The young Friedrich Engels in his 1844 study *The Condition of the Working Class in England* provides what is still the best description of how the new world of industrial capitalism turned the lives of working men and women upside-down:

> All conceivable evils are heaped upon the heads of the poor. If the population of great cities is too dense in general, it is they in particular who are packed into the least space. As though the vitiated atmosphere of the streets were not enough, they are penned in dozens into single rooms, so that the air which they breathe at night in itself is enough to stifle them... They are supplied bad, tattered or rotten clothing, adulterated and indigestible food. They are exposed to the most exciting changes of mental condition, the most violent vibrations between hope and fear; they are hunted like game, and not permitted to attain peace of mind and quiet enjoyment of life. They are deprived of all enjoyments except that of sexual indulgence and drunkenness, are worked every day to the point of complete exhaustion of their mental and physical energies, and are thus constantly spurred on in the only two enjoyments at their command. And if they surmount all this, they fall victims to want of work in a crisis when all the little is taken from them that had hitherto been vouchsafed them.[45]

Given such living conditions, alongside the inability of families to care for their unwell members, it is hardy surprising that many workers succumbed both to alcoholism and to conditions such as syphilis, which were among the most common reasons for admission to the new asylums.

Finally, the optimistic ideas that madness could be cured which flourished in the decades following the French Revolution had given way by the end of the 19th century to a therapeutic pessimism which saw madness as a "crushing life sentence" from which there could be no respite, a view also underpinned by eugenic ideas about the hereditary nature of madness, which was seen as particularly affecting the working class. In his 1894 address to the forerunner of the American Psychiatric Association, the eminent neurologist Silas Weir Mitchell attacked that pessimism and castigated those present for presiding over what he called:

> A collection of "living corpses", pathetic patients "who have lost even the memory of hope, [and] sit in rows, too dull to know despair, watched by attendants: silent, grewsome [sic] machines which eat and sleep, sleep and eat".[46]

## Psychiatry's horrible histories

> It is around 25 years since I sat waiting in an ante-room within a gigantic British mental institution, where the adoptive mother who had reared me from early infancy lay in a condition of passive dementia. When it was time for me to enter the ward, the nurse in charge drew from her pocket a bunch of keys, and unlocked the door into a large hall, filled with row upon row of beds, in one of which, scarcely recognisable, lay my parent. The keys tinkled in the silence of that corridor; and it is still easy for me to hear the sound of their metal. It is a sound that reverberates back over the centuries of locked doors and futile dormitories of the neglected. In physical material terms the locks have all but gone; but in these matters the human mind still finds it hard to unlock itself.[47]

When compared with Silas Weir Mitchell's comments above, Peter Sedgwick's poignant reminiscence of his adoptive mother's experience in a 1950s British mental asylum highlights how little had changed in the care of those with mental health problems over the preceding half century. The therapeutic pessimism to which Mitchell referred was, if anything, even more pronounced by the early 1950s.

That was not to say there were no challenges to the dominant psychiatric ideas during this time. The "shell-shock" experienced by many First World War soldiers, for example, (what today would be called post-traumatic stress disorder) and even more so by middle class officers such as the poet Siegfried Sassoon, challenged hereditary theories of mental disorder and lent support to the idea that this condition might be an involuntary psychological reaction to the horrors of war, rather than simply a way of avoiding fighting (though that of course, did not prevent more than 300 British soldiers being executed as deserters).

Thus, a minority of psychiatrists argued for a more humane response, usually involving the use of talking therapies, in place of the brutal and punitive behaviourist "treatments" employed up till then. (The psychiatric practices and debates of the period are powerfully described in Pat Barker's novel *Regeneration*). Similarly the period following the Second World War saw the development by psychotherapists such as Maxwell Jones and Wilfred Bion of more democratic and collective approaches to the treatment of mental health problems, including group therapy and the therapeutic communities set up by Jones at Dingleton Hospital in Scotland and elsewhere as a conscious political and therapeutic response to the fascist ideologies of the 1930s.

Far from progressive, however, were some of the other practices employed by psychiatrists across Europe and the USA in the first half of the 20th century, working consciously or otherwise at the behest of their particular ruling class. Space does not permit a full discussion here of the often brutal practices carried out on mainly working class men and women in the name of "treatment"[48] but a few examples will give a flavour of what was involved.

Mention has been made above of the role of psychiatry in coercing soldiers back into the trenches during the First World War. Scull gives a graphic description of the way in which psychiatrists from all sides of the conflict dealt with soldiers exhibiting symptoms of shell shock and unwilling to fight:

> Separately, and apparently independently, German, Austrian, French and British psychiatrists made use of powerful electric currents to inflict great pain on their patients in an effort to force them to abandon their symptoms, to get the mute to speak, the deaf to hear, the lame to walk. Most famous among the Germans was Fritz Kaufmann (1875-1941), inventor of the Kaufman cure, which combined intensely painful electric shocks applied to apparently paralysed limbs for hours at a time, with shouted commands to perform military drills. The aim was to get the patient to give in, abandon his attachment to his symptoms, and be ready to return to the killing fields.[49]

Shocking as Kaufmann's methods were, as Scull notes, French and British psychiatrists "enthusiastically made use of exactly the same approach", not least because whatever sympathy they possessed lay mainly with the views of their military superiors.

The decades following the First World War saw the development of a range of physical treatments which, well-intentioned or not, also inflicted great suffering on individuals who were already extremely distressed. These included the deliberate infection of patients with malaria as a cure for Generalised Paralysis of the Insane, caused by syphilis; surgery on patients (including removal of organs) in the belief that mental illness was rooted in chronic infections in different parts of the body; insulin coma therapy; the use of electro-convulsive therapy (ECT); and the widespread use of psychosurgery (lobotomy and leucotomy). By 1951, more than 18, 000 patients in the US had undergone lobotomy. While debates continue over the effectiveness or otherwise of ECT in treating depression, most of these brutal and damaging "treatments" have long been consigned to the dustbin of history.

## Psychiatry under the Nazis

On a different scale altogether, however, was what leading British psychiatrist Tom Burns has called "undoubtedly [psychiatry's] most shameful chapter"—namely the profession's involvement in Aktion T4, the systematic extermination by the Nazis of around 70,000 mentally ill and learning disabled individuals in Germany, a figure that had risen to around 200, 000 by the end of the Second World War.[50]

> The terrible shame of the extermination of the mentally ill is compounded by several prominent psychiatrists leading it and none vigorously opposing it... The broad mass of the profession probably did not share the extreme views articulated, but they voiced no effective opposition. Psychiatry was no better than those around it and, arguably in this instance, worse. There is no excuse.[51]

As Burns correctly argues, one reason for that collusion was a eugenicist ideology, then highly influential both within psychiatry and in the wider society, which saw people with mental health problems and learning disabilities as "degenerate", their lives not worth living. Another was the desire for political and professional respectability and acceptance. Also important, however, was the profession's view of itself as above politics, as motivated by purely scientific concerns with a consequent refusal to address its political role as an instrument of social control, particularly of poor people, ethnic minorities and women. The narrow positivist view of science which prevailed within psychiatry in the 1930s undoubtedly made it easier for psychiatrists to deny or ignore the ethical and political implications of cooperation with the Nazis. In this they were not alone. Writing about the equally shameful collusion of the German social work profession and the involvement of many of its members in the assessment of people with mental health problems or learning disabilities as suitable for sterilisation or worse, the historian of European social work Walter Lorenz has written:

> Sticking to their professional task with the air of value neutrality and scientific detachment (especially after the "non-conforming", "politically active" social workers had been sacked or imprisoned), they did not feel responsible for the consequences of their assessments and indeed may not have been conscious of the full implications their work had in the national context.[52]

Such "horrible histories" raise difficult questions about the nature of psychiatry as a profession. As Peter Sedgwick noted, there has been a long-running debate among critics of psychiatry between those who view the kind of episodes described above as stemming from the *abuse* of psychiatric power and methods—who believe in other words, that a humane psychiatry is possible—and those who see such oppression and abuses as inherent in a professional project which locates mental distress in biomedical theories of the mind.[53] In this connection it is worth noting that there have been different traditions within psychiatry, some more progressive than others. As well as the psychoanalytic approaches discussed in the next chapter and the anti-psychiatry movement of the 1960s and 1970s discussed in Chapter 4, there is also the social psychiatry movement of the post-World War Two period referred to above and present-day movements such as the Critical Psychiatry Network (as well as radical pioneers such as the Swiss psychiatrist Eugen Bleuler).

That said, there is little reason to believe that the positivist view of science which prevailed in earlier decades and which sees natural science methods as wholly applicable to human minds is any less influential today than it was in the 1930s. Here, for example, are two leading British psychiatrists writing in the mid-1970s, critiquing the view, by then widely accepted, that mental distress was rooted in people's relationships and life experiences and that psychiatrists and others needed to take seriously the voices of people with mental health problems:

Today, it is assumed that mental pathology derives from normal psychology and can be understood in terms of faulty inter or intrapersonal relationships and corrected by re-education or psychoanalysis of where the patient's emotional development went wrong. Despite all efforts which have gone into this approach and all the reams devoted to it, results have been meager not to say inconclusive, and contrast sharply with what medicine has given to psychiatry and which is added to year by year. [This is because] patients are victims of their brain rather than their mind. *To reap the rewards of this medical approach, however, means a reorientation of psychiatry, from listening to looking.*[54]

In truth, with the (possible) exception of psychoanalysis which will be discussed in Chapter 3 (and which has never been the dominant discourse in British adult psychiatry), seriously listening to the voices and experiences of people with mental health problems (as opposed to gathering data to form the basis of a diagnosis) has arguably never been at the forefront of psychiatric practice. The more common patient experience has been one of not being listened to and of views and experiences being discounted or invalidated. In his history of madness, Porter cites the experiences of two patients in British asylums, more than 100 years apart. The first, John Perceval, son of the assassinated Prime Minister Spencer Perceval, wrote the following in 1838 in a memoir described by Porter as "perhaps the most perceptive and poignant account ever written by an ex-patient about asylum life":

Men acted as though my body, soul and spirit were fairly given up to their control, to work their mischief and folly upon. My silence, I suppose, gave consent. I mean, that I was never told, such and such things we are going to do; we think it advisable to administer such and such medicine, in this or that manner; I was never asked, Do you want any thing? Do you wish for, prefer, any thing? Have you any objection to this or that?

Some 120 years later, an exposé of conditions in British psychiatric hospitals in the 1950s written by two Members of Parliament (MPs) contained the following account by a former inmate:

I was not allowed to write to my best friend to tell her where to locate me… [T]he staff ignored me… I thought this technique must be a new method for the study of mental illness; but I was soon to learn that it appeared to be nothing but a callous belief that the insane do not suffer and that any problems they express are bound to be "imaginary".[55]

Nor were such experiences untypical. As Scull comments:

> Morally, socially and physically removed from the ranks of humankind, locked up in institutions impervious to the gaze of outsiders, deprived of their status as moral actors, and presumed by virtue of their mental state to lack the capacity to make informed choices for themselves, patients were mostly unable to resist those who controlled their very existence, though some managed to do so.[56]

It was that extreme powerlessness, characteristic of what Erving Goffman in his celebrated 1961 work *Asylums* referred to as "total institutions", combined with a view that the lives and voices of the mentally unwell were worth less (as well, no doubt, as a hefty dose of racism) that led to "experiments" such as that at the Tuskegee Asylum in Alabama where over a 40-year period between 1932 and the early 1970s around 600 black men were used as guinea pigs, without their knowledge or consent, in an experiment to test long-term responses to syphilis, in what was, in Roy Porter's words, "a minor echo of the atrocities committed by Nazi psychiatrists".[57]

## From the asylum to DSM-5

Asylum populations in the UK and the USA peaked in the mid-1950s and declined rapidly thereafter. In Britain, the total number of available mental hospital beds (for all ages and for all specialities) dropped from a peak of roughly 150,000 beds in 1955 to around 22,300 in 2012. Different explanations have been put forward to account for this dramatic fall. Initial beliefs that it was due to the discovery and introduction of new anti-psychotic drugs such as Largactil (chlorpromazine) for people with conditions such as schizophrenia have been largely discounted, both on grounds of timing (the decline in numbers had begun before the new treatments were introduced) and also because some of the biggest falls involved older people who by and large did not receive that medication. Andrew Scull, one of the leading authorities on this issue, concludes:

[A] variety of scholars who have systematically reviewed the available evidence have arrived at similar conclusions: the influence of the new drugs on deinstitutionalisation was at best indirect and limited, and conscious shifts in social policy were far more important determinants of the emptying of mental hospitals.[58]

These shifts in social policy were themselves the product of economic, ideological and political pressures. Economically, while the "fiscal crisis" argument put forward by Scull—the view that the cutback in hospital provision took place primarily for financial reasons—is less convincing in respect of the earlier period of deinstitutionalisation in the 1950s, when capitalism in both the USA and Britain was expanding, fiscal considerations and a commitment to a smaller state were certainly important drivers of the 1962 Hospital Plan put forward by right wing Conservative MP and Tory Health Minister Enoch Powell which proclaimed the closure of the asylums in the UK. The argument for fiscal factors becomes even more convincing from the mid-1970s onwards, when the global economy was shrinking and a new ideology—initially known as monetarism, then neoliberalism—was taking hold. It was in this later period, for example, that some of the biggest reductions in provision took place, with a 39 percent reduction in the number of inpatient psychiatric beds in England between 1998 and 2012.[59]

Ideological factors were also important in the dismantling of the asylum and the promotion of "community care". And as Peter Sedgwick commented, here ideology was deployed in the classic Marxist sense:

Not to reflect or communicate ideas about reality but on the contrary to act as a smokescreen, masking the bitter facts of social oppression in the self-interest of a powerful and articulate minority. In Britain, no less than in the United States, "community care" and "the replacement of the mental hospital" were slogans which masked the growing depletion of real services for mental patients; the accumulating numbers of impaired, retarded and demented males in the prisons and common lodging-houses; the scarcity not only of local authority residential provision for the mentally-disabled but of day centres and skilled social work resources; the jettisoning of mental patients in their thousands into the isolated, helpless environment of their families of origin, who appealed in vain for hospital admission (or even temporary respite), for counselling or support, and even for basic information about the patient's diagnosis and medication.[60]

Scull makes a similar point in relation to deinstitutionalisation policy in Italy:

[A]s was also the case everywhere, the Italians has closed their mental hospitals without troubling to provide alternative structures to handle the problems posed by serious mental illness. Much of the burden was displaced on to families and they have been vociferous about the social difficulties they are confronted with. Other patients were simply moved from public mental hospitals to private residential facilities, about which the authorities profess to know little. Still others find themselves in prison or on the street... Community care was a shell game with no pea.[61]

Both Sedgwick and Scull were pointing to a dilemma which continues to challenge mental health campaigners—that for all their faults and limitations, the alternatives to traditional mental health services on offer from governments committed to reducing state expenditure and increasing the role of the private sector in health and social care are frequently even less palatable than existing services.

That dilemma was obscured by the fact that much of the criticism both of the asylum and of psychiatry was driven by humanitarian concerns for the recipients of psychiatric treatments, often coming from the left. Novels such as Sylvia Plath's *The Bell Jar* and movies such as *One Flew Over the Cuckoo's Nest* (based on Ken Kesey's novel of the same name) savaged not just the asylum but also the practice of psychiatrists. Above all, there was the movement in the 1960s known as "anti-psychiatry", based on the ideas of a collection of disparate thinkers including the Scottish psychiatrist R D Laing, sociologists Michel Foucault and Erving Goffman, and the American psychiatrist Thomas Szasz and which will be discussed in Chapter 4.

A key plank of the critique of psychiatry at that time concerned the validity of its diagnoses. One academic study which contributed significantly to that critique was based on a series of experiments conducted by psychologist David Rosenhan, a Stanford University professor, and published by the journal *Science* in 1973 under the title

"On being sane in insane places". Rosenhan's study was carried out in two parts. The first part involved the use of healthy associates or "pseudopatients" (three women and five men, including Rosenhan himself) who briefly feigned auditory hallucinations in an attempt to gain admission to 12 different psychiatric hospitals in five different states in various locations in the USA. All were admitted and diagnosed with psychiatric disorders. After admission, the pseudopatients acted normally and told staff that they felt fine and no longer experienced any additional hallucinations. All were forced to admit to having a mental illness and to agree to take antipsychotic drugs as a condition of their release. The average time that the patients spent in the hospital was 19 days. All but one were diagnosed with schizophrenia "in remission" before their release.

The second part of his study involved one offended hospital administration challenging Rosenhan to send pseudopatients to its facility, whom staff would then detect. Rosenhan agreed and in the following weeks out of 193 new patients the staff identified 41 as potential pseudopatients, with 19 of these receiving suspicion from at least one psychiatrist and one other staff member. In fact, Rosenhan had sent no one to the hospital.[62]

The challenge to psychiatry, however, was not confined to academic researchers. In the same year in which Rosenhan's paper appeared, a campaign by gay activists succeeded in persuading the American Psychiatric Association to remove homosexuality from the psychiatrists' "bible", the DSM (the Diagnostic and Statistical Manual of Mental Disorders], where it had been classified as a mental illness. The effect of this, coupled with Rosenhan's experiments and coming on the back of mounting criticism of mainstream psychiatry over the previous decade, was, in the words of one critic:

> To reveal that even when psychiatrists did agree on a diagnosis, they might have been diagnosing something that wasn't an illness. Or, to put it another way, psychiatrists didn't seem to know the difference between sickness and health.[63]

Rosenhan's study concluded: "it is clear that we cannot distinguish the sane from the insane in psychiatric hospitals" and also highlighted the dangers of dehumanisation and labelling in psychiatric institutions.

## DSM: the medicalisation of everyday life

The response of the psychiatric profession (or rather, its leading section in the form of the American Psychiatric Association) to critiques which challenged all aspects of the psychiatric enterprise, above all the notion that there was a biological basis for most forms of mental distress, came in the form of DSM-III, published in 1980.

Versions of the Diagnostic and Statistical Manual of Mental Disorders, which provided psychiatrists with classifications of mental disorders, had been around since the early 1950s. DSM-III differed however in two key respects. Firstly, and most obviously, it was much bigger. Whereas DSM-I, published in 1952, was 130 pages long and listed 106 disorders, DSM-III was 494 pages and listed 265 diagnostic categories (continuing that trend, DSM-IV, published in 1994, ran to 886 pages with 297 disorders).

Secondly, the primary concern of its authors was to overcome the lack of consistency in diagnosis exposed by experiments such as Rosenhan's. For its key author, leading psychiatrist Robert Spitzer, that meant abandoning the fuzzy psychoanalytic clinical understandings that had shaped the DSM and US psychiatry until then and returning to the observational approach pioneered by one of the founding fathers of psychiatry in the late 19th century, Emil Kraepelin. "Psychiatry", Spitzer informed author and psychotherapist Gary Greenberg "was regarded as bogus… I knew it would be better off if it was accepted as a medical discipline".[64] In practice that meant abandoning any pretence at under-standing the origins and nature of mental illness and, like Kraepelin, focusing on the one thing that psychiatrists could claim to know: what they could observe. That meant producing checklists of symptoms for particular conditions, such as depression or schizophrenia. In the case of depression, for example, if five out of eight symptoms were present (such as sleep difficulties, loss of interest in usual activities, poor appetite and so on) then a diagnosis of depression was warranted.

It was a method which would leave much less room for disagree-ment. There was, however, a major flaw in this approach, noted by Greenberg and of which Spitzer was aware. For while the revised DSM significantly improved *reliability*—the extent to which the diagnostic criteria would yield agreement among clinicians—it did nothing to address the issue of *validity*—the extent to which the diagnosis described an actual disease. Nevertheless, as Greenberg comments:

Spitzer had fashioned a dictionary of disorder that allowed psychiatrists to identify our foibles without recourse to the troublesome mumbo jumbo, or for that matter, any other mumbo jumbo. And the result was sensational. The DSM-III not only restored both internal and external confidence in psychiatry: it was also an international bestseller.[65]

The impact of the DSM (the fifth version of which was published in 2013) has been massive, both materially and ideologically. Materially, the huge proliferation in diagnoses has been of massive benefit to a pharmaceutical industry keen to market a drug for every new condition. It has also led to much closer cooperation between psychiatrists and these drug companies. While activists and critical sociologists in the 1960s used to refer to the "military-industrial complex", critics of psychiatry now refer to what Peter Breggin has termed the "psychopharmaceutical complex".

Some sense of the degree of collusion that exists between psychiatry and "Big Pharma" is shown by the fact that of the authors who selected and defined the DSM-IV psychiatric disorders, roughly half have had financial relationships with the pharmaceutical industry at one time, raising the prospect of a direct conflict of interest.[66] The connections between panel members involved in contributing to the DSM and the drug companies were particularly strong in those diagnoses where drugs are the first line of treatment, such as schizophrenia and mood disorders, where 100 percent of the panel members had financial ties with the pharmaceutical industry. The DSM is also one of the major sources of income of the American Psychiatric Association, earning it over US$100 million a year.

Ideologically the DSM has contributed to the medicalisation of human nature and everyday life. One of the proposed changes in the decade-long revision of DSM-IV and the preparation of DSM-5, for example, was to make ordinary grief a mental disorder. According to Dr Allen Frances, the editor of DSM-IV (1994) but one of the main critics of the proliferation of new psychiatric categories proposed for DSM-5:

> Reclassifying bereavement as a symptom of depression will not only increase the rates of unnecessary medication...but also reduces the sanctity of bereavement as a mammalian and human condition.[67]

Several other proposed inclusions also worried Frances. Interviewed by the writer James Davies, author of *Cracked: Why Psychiatry is Doing More Harm Than Good*, he argued:

> [T]here is the new "generalised anxiety disorder" which threatens to turn the aches and pains and disappointments of everyday life into mental illness. There is "minor neurocognitive disorder" that will likely turn the normal forgetting of ageing into a mental illness. There is the "disruptive mood dysregulation disorder" which will see children's temper tantrums become symptoms of disorder. These changes will expand the definition of mental illnesses to include more people, exposing more to potentially dangerous medications.[68]

Similar concerns were expressed in an online petition in 2012 protesting against the proposed additions to DSM-5 and supported by more than 50 mental health organisations including the British Psychological Society, the Danish Psychological Society and the American Counselling Association. Like Frances, these organisations were concerned that lowering the diagnostic thresholds for a disorder would mean more people would be unnecessarily labelled unwell and an increase in inappropriate treatment of vulnerable populations, including children and old people; and that by de-emphasising the socio-cultural causes of suffering, biological causes would continue to be wrongly privileged. As the petition concluded:

> In the light of growing empirical evidence that neurobiology does not fully account for the emergence of mental distress, as well as new longitudinal studies revealing long-term hazards of psychotropic treatment, we believe that these changes pose substantial risks to patients/clients, practitioners and the mental health professions in general.[69]

In arguing against the privileging of biological causes and the downplaying of social factors in the onset of mental health problems, the petition is evidence of the growing desire on the part of many service users, social workers and clinical psychologists as well as a minority of psychiatrists to move beyond the currently dominant biomedical model or paradigm.

One reason for dissatisfaction with that paradigm already referred to above is the lack of precision or validity of key psychiatric categories such as schizophrenia (which is not the same as saying that the symptoms associated with these conditions, such as hearing voices, are not "real" or are not distressing).

A second source of dissatisfaction is the overemphasis on weak biological explanations, including genetic explanations. These may or may not at some point in the future yield new understandings of, or treatments for, mental health problems, but at the expense of addressing in the here and now social and economic factors such as poverty and inequality for which there is already strong evidence of a causal link. As Richard Bentall argues:

> [S]ubstantial resources have been spent, and continue to be spent, in the attempt to discover the genetic origins of mental illness, whereas its social origins continue to be neglected... In this context, it is important to note that no patient, not a single one, has ever benefitted from genetic research into mental illness, although many may have been indirectly harmed by it (because it has discouraged the development of adequate services for patients and in one shameful period, was used to justify their slaughter)... Indeed, from the point of view of patients, there can be few other areas of medical research that have yielded such a dismal return for effort expended.[70]

A third reason for dissatisfaction is the growing evidence that despite the inflated claims made for them by pharmaceutical companies, very often the drugs don't work. In respect of anti-depressants, for example, as one group of psychiatrists argued in a guest editorial in the *British Journal of Psychiatry*:

> There is strong evidence that improvement in depression comes mainly from non-technical aspects of interventions. Recent meta-analyses of drug treatments for depression demonstrate that drug–placebo differences are minimal.
>
> Even in subgroups of individuals who are more severely depressed, where differences have been reported as being clinically significant, they are still small in absolute terms and may be simply the result of decreased responsiveness to placebo... Overall, available evidence does not support the idea that antidepressants work by correcting a pre-existing "chemical imbalance".[71]

Why then, given this weak evidence for biological factors as causes of mental health issues and the effectiveness of drug treatments on the one hand and the very strong evidence for social factors on the other, do drug interventions continue to be far and away the main way in which society responds to mental distress?

A large part of the answer lies in the fact that, as Bentall has succinctly observed, "there's gold in them thar pills". The pharmaceutical industry is, in fact, the most profitable industry in the world:

> [B]y the beginning of the twenty-first century, the top ten companies were making an 18.5 percent return on sales, compared to an average return for other industries of 3.3 percent. Even commercial banking could not equal this level of profit, making a return of 13.5 percent. By 2002, the combined profits for the top ten drug companies in the Fortune 500 (a list of 500 American corporations with the highest gross revenues) had grown to exceed the profits of all the other 490 put together.[72]

And it is such capitalist competition, rather than a humanitarian or altruistic concern to alleviate mental suffering, that drives the increasing medicalisation of everyday life:

> When considering the role of the pharmaceutical industry in psychiatric research, it is important to recognise that the industry's main purpose is to make money for its shareholders. Drug companies are no more driven by the desire to do good than the manufacturers of automobiles, canned soup or other household products... [T]hey are willing to use any and every method to promote their products to the citizens of the industrialised nations, who have learned (or been taught) to look to the medical profession for solutions to a wide range of physical, social and existential ills.[73]

### Where now for the medical model of mental health?

How, then, have defenders of psychiatry responded to these critiques of their professional knowledge and practice? Here, two recent responses will be considered.

In *Our Necessary Shadow: the Nature and Meaning of Psychiatry*, Tom Burns, Professor of Social Psychiatry at the University of Oxford, has sought to provide an up to date understanding of "what psychiatry is, what it can do and what it cannot do". Burns begins by acknowledging the contested and lowly status of psychiatry, both among the general public and also within the medical profession. He cites Andrew Scull:

Reflecting the poverty of its cognitive accomplishments, its persistently dismal therapeutic capacities, and the social undesirability and disreputability of most of its clientele, psychiatry has enjoyed a perpetually marginal and unenviable position in the social division of labour—a profession always, so it seems, but a step away from a profound crisis of legitimacy.[74]

Burns' response to such criticisms is to accept most of them but nevertheless to continue to assert the value of psychiatry and of the medical model on which it rests (albeit redefined by him to place greater emphasis on the importance of relationships). The tone of the book is well captured in an early assertion about the value of psychiatry:

Psychiatry has made many mistakes and will continue to make further mistakes. I hope, however, that recognition of the massive good that it does, and a fuller understanding of the constraints under which it has to operate, will put these failings in perspective. Most people who consult a psychiatrist benefit from the encounter; they get relief from often intolerable symptoms. The relief may not be permanent but it is much appreciated and for some it is life-saving.[75]

The mistakes, as well as some of the "horrible histories" of psychiatry have been considered above. The central issue, of course, is not about the reality of emotional and psychological pain, but whether there might be other, better ways of understanding and addressing it than those currently provided by mainstream psychiatry.

Burns' book inadvertently highlights the contradictions inherent in psychiatry's knowledge base. On the one hand, the current authority of psychiatry rests on its association with medicine and its adherence to a theoretical model which insists there are discrete mental conditions or illnesses (depression, anxiety, schizophrenia, etc) whose origins are located in the brain. On the other hand, as Burns argues, psychiatry in practice is often an essentially pragmatic, atheoretical exercise:

Psychiatrists broadly share the same approach to their task as the nurses, psychologists and social workers that they work with, but they have a special responsibility for the "medical model". In essence, the medical model is a very practical approach to treatment with a little emphasis on theory ("if it works, keep doing it, if it doesn't work, stop doing it"). Psychiatrists do, of course, use theories to structure their thinking and guide what they do, but they are not restricted to any one theory. There is no "-ology" for psychiatry. For different patients (or even for the same patient at different times) they may rely on biology, pharmacology, psychology, physiology or sociology. They draw on whatever seems most helpful there and then.[76]

A similarly pragmatic justification for the continued use of the medical model in psychiatry is put by two other psychiatrists, Premal Shah and Deborah Mountain, in a 2007 article in the *British Journal of Psychiatry* entitled "The medical model is dead—long live the medical model":

> We believe that we need a simple definition of the medical model, which incorporates medicine's fundamental ideals, to facilitate clarity and precision, without denying its shortcomings. We propose that the "medical model" is a process whereby, informed by the best available evidence, doctors advise on, coordinate or deliver interventions for health improvement. It can be summarily stated as "does it work?"[77]

Clearly both sets of authors believe that by sidestepping the "ideological" issues around psychiatry, they have provided a strong common sense justification for the use of the medical model in psychiatry. In reality, they have done the opposite.

Firstly, the "what works" argument in this sphere is open to the same objections as What Works, a New Labour policy pioneered in every area of social policy, more generally. Above all, *for whom* does it work? It could be argued, for example, that from the UK government's point of view, the Work Capability Assessment, reinforced in some areas by the use of cognitive behavioural therapy (CBT), to coerce people back into work—what has been described as "psycho-compulsion"—"works", is a success, in the sense that fewer people with mental health problems now claim benefit. Money has been saved. The cost, however, has been much higher levels of stress and a rise in the suicide rate, hardly a "success" for those affected and their families.

Secondly, what is to count as evidence? Numerous studies, for example, have shown that people with mental health problems would like more access to talking therapies and different forms of social support. Do service users' views count as evidence or is evidence confined to data collected from randomised control trials?

Thirdly, the suggestion that the methods employed by psychiatrists are driven primarily by the best available evidence is scarcely convincing. In addition to the evidence presented above regarding the effectiveness or otherwise of psychiatric drugs, consider also the example of ECT. While some people, particularly those experiencing very severe depression, have undoubtedly found ECT helpful, many others have not, complaining of damaging side effects including memory loss. In an attempt to resolve the issue, the 18 members of the Food and Drug Administration's Neurological Devices Advisory Panel in the USA met in 2011 to decide whether to classify ECT machines as "high risk":

> The Panel was presented with 3,045 written submissions and a 154-page "FDA Executive Summary" of the research…and listened to two days of verbal submissions. After all this, they voted 10 to 8 that ECT should be classified as "high-risk" for people with depression and (somewhat illogically) by greater margins for other diagnoses eg 13 to 4 for schizophrenia.[78]

Despite that powerful and influential evidence, however, in 2017 the use of ECT is once more on the rise in England:

> Exclusive data covering four-fifths of NHS mental health trusts in England shows that more than 22,600 individual ECT treatments were carried out in 2015-16, a rise of 11 percent from four years ago, when about 20,400 were carried out.
>
> The number of patients treated also rose, albeit more modestly, to more than 2,200, suggesting that on average individuals undergo more ECT procedures than before.[79]

While it is possible or even likely that increased use of ECT is a reflection of both aspects of the crisis in mental health discussed in the previous chapter (a rise in levels of depression coupled with the reduction of community-based services), it hardly supports the argument that the case for the medical model is its reliance on evidence-based practice.

Finally, Burns' fall-back position is to stress the centrality of relationships in mental health treatment. He argues that: "I also learnt over years that relationships are key". In one respect, here he is on stronger ground. There is substantial research evidence from different disciplines that suggests that it is the quality of the worker/client relationship, rather than the specific therapy employed, that facilitates therapeutic change. But that position also poses two problems for those who wish to defend the medical model.

First, among psychiatrists, Burns is very much in a minority. Within the profession, and especially in its most powerful section in the USA, the argument that mental health problems have their roots in biology is stronger than ever. Second, few psychiatrists could claim that either their training or their knowledge base gives them a specific expertise in relationship-based work. In fact their skills in this area are likely to be no better than those of other professional colleagues such as psychotherapists, counsellors or social workers. Seeking to rescue psychiatry by emphasising the importance of relationships to mental health is therefore potentially a double-edged sword.

# 3

# "Neuroses are social diseases":[80] Marxism and psychoanalysis

## Introduction

For several decades following the Second World War, the dominant way of understanding mental health and mental health problems, especially in the USA, was provided not by biomedical psychiatry but by psychoanalysis, the theory and practice founded around the turn of the 20th century by Sigmund Freud. Most American psychiatrists were trained analysts and psychoanalytic concepts underpinned the early editions of the DSM. The influence of psychoanalysis, however, was felt far beyond the consulting room. Its assumptions pervaded every aspect of daily life, partly through the publications of texts sympathetic to Freudian ideas such as Erich Fromm's *The Art of Loving* which became a best-seller, both in the USA and globally.

While a minority of Marxists including Fromm himself and Herbert Marcuse continued to defend what they saw (albeit very differently) as Freud's radical legacy, they both recognised there was very little that was progressive about the conformist psychoanalysis which dominated in the post-war period. In respect of gay men and lesbians, for example, before the early 1980s some 500 psychoanalytic essays and books had been written on the topic of homosexuality. Of these, "less than half a dozen clamed homosexuality might be part of a satisfactory psychic organisation".[81]

Similarly, discussing the contribution of psychoanalysis to women's oppression in post-war America, Betty Freidan wrote:

> Freud was accepted so quickly and completely at the end of the forties that for over a decade no one even questioned the race of the educated American woman back to the home... After the depression, after the war, Freudian psychology became much more than a science of human behaviour, a therapy for the suffering. It became an all-embracing

America ideology, a new religion...Freudian and pseudo-Freudian theories settled everywhere, like fine volcanic ash.[82]

Nor did transgender people fare better. As Laura Miles has noted:

In the eyes of most of the sexologists, doctors and campaigners of this period up until the mid-20th century gender variant behaviour remained essentially undifferentiated from homosexuality. Someone who expressed the desire to "change sex" was generally regarded as a homosexual unable to face up to their homosexuality—a "self-denying homosexual". Many Freudians persisted in that view for decades after the notion of the transsexual became differentiated from the homosexual. The term transsexual did not really emerge as a medical or social category, or a self-identification in more general use, until after the publication of Harry Benjamin's book, *The Transsexual Phenomenon*, in 1966.[83]

In the UK, psychoanalysis had less impact on adult psychiatry but did exert a considerable influence in other areas of mental health care such as child guidance and social work, partly through the writings of a distinguished group of analysts based in Britain which included Freud's daughter Anna Freud, Melanie Klein, Donald Winnicott and John Bowlby.

Psychoanalysis has largely fallen out of favour within both clinical psychology and psychiatry. For the most part, the former bases its research and practice methods on the empirical model of the natural sciences, the latter, as we saw in the previous chapter, is increasingly rooted in biomedicine. Both also draw heavily on developments within neuroscience. Where psychoanalytic ideas do continue to flourish, however, is within the humanities departments of universities, particularly in literature departments and on film and media courses, partly through the work of writers such as Jacqueline Rose and Slavoj Žižek. More generally, as Stephen Frosh has noted, Western culture continues to be permeated by psychoanalytic ideas. The notion, for example, that childhood strongly influences adulthood is very widely accepted, while

[t]he central psychoanalytic notion that we have unconscious motivations that drive our behaviour and are often not understood by us is perhaps just as pervasive. When people ask of themselves why they did something, or accuse a friend of self-deception, or of not being able to see the "real" reasons for their actions, they are drawing on what can be

called a psychoanalytic "discourse" to make sense of their social environment. This suggests that culture is "saturated" by psychoanalytic assumptions in ways that are not obvious because they are so taken-for-granted.[84]

In a recent example, former Clinton adviser Sydney Blumenthal, referring to Donald Trump's habit of disinhibited tweeting at all hours of the day and night in response to perceived slights or insults, has spoken of "his id's unfiltered outlet, his trigger-happy twitter account".[85]

For much of the post-war period, however, with some exceptions, psychoanalysis has not been central to the concerns of Marxists and the left more generally (the exceptions being France after 1968, Latin America, and the discipline of cultural studies referred to above). At best, it has been seen as simply not relevant to the task of developing a theory and practice which can contribute to the overthrow of capitalism. At worst, it has been viewed as a speculative, unscientific worldview which is biologically reductionist, overemphasises the role of sexuality in shaping behaviour and individualises forms of mental distress which are in reality the product of a society based on oppression, exploitation and alienation.

Not infrequently, the criticism is directed primarily at its founder. The British critical psychologist David Smail, for example, has suggested that Freud's abandonment of the "seduction theory" (the theory that neurosis was the product of trauma, of actual rape or abuse rather than childhood fantasy) was driven primarily by his (unconscious) desire to make more money:

> Could it be that Freud's gradual shifting of the blame for his patients' "neuroses" from the fathers and uncles of his "hysterical" female patients to, eventually, themselves…might have something to do with who was paying his bills?[86]

There are valid criticisms that can be made of Freud and of psychoanalysis from a Marxist standpoint, some of which will be considered below. That said, there has always been a minority current within Marxism which has sought to find common ground between these two intellectual traditions. That certainly was the approach of some leading Marxists in the period when psychoanalysis was being developed, most famously Leon Trotsky. Defending Freud's Russian followers in 1926 when the Party under Stalin's leadership was beginning to move against them, Trotsky argued that:

> It would be too simple and crude to declare psychoanalysis as incompatible with Marxism and to turn one's back on it. In any case, we are not obliged to adopt Freudianism either. It is a working hypothesis. It can produce, and it does produce deductions and surmises which point to a materialist psychology. In due time, experimentation will provide the tests. Meanwhile, we have neither reason nor right to declare a ban on a method which, even though it may be less reliable, tries to anticipate results towards which the experimental method advances only very slowly.[87]

Similarly, writing in 1960 the philosopher Alasdair McIntyre, at that time a revolutionary Marxist and editor of the journal *International Socialism*, described Freud as "one of the two greatest thinkers of our age" who saw "in the rational comprehension of desire the path to freedom".[88] More recently, Marxists such as Terry Eagleton and Alex Callinicos have also written favourably, if critically, of the subversive potential of psychoanalytic thought.

As all of these writers recognise, the roots of Freud's radicalism, in common with thinkers such as Hegel and Darwin, do not lie in the overt political positions he espoused. He was a liberal who, like Thomas Hobbes three centuries earlier, had a very negative and individualistic view of human nature, seeing people as essentially aggressive and self-centred. To that extent, he believed that a degree of repression was necessary if civilisation was to survive. At the same time, however, he was by no means an uncritical supporter of Western civilisation and could see in his patients the enormous suffering which repression, especially sexual repression, was producing. Herein lies his radical edge. As Russell Jacoby notes:

> To be sure, Freud cannot simply be categorised as a cultural or sexual radical. Nevertheless a reforming and social impulse unmistakeably ran through many of his texts. This impulse permeated the psychoanalytic movement, attracting and sustaining individuals unhappy with the sexual and social codes of the day.[89]

Similarly, Jonathon Lear suggests that instead of reading Freud's critique of civilisation and the individual's discontent as a timeless account of an inevitable tragic conflict between individual and society, read it as pointing out a *fault-line*—a place where the needs of the individual and the aims to which society tends come into conflict. One can then read Freud as providing the material for a political critique of the conditions of bourgeois modernity. That is, one can read him as making the historical claim that in the social conditions in which he encountered his patients, the discrepancy between the conditions needed for humans to flourish and the demands imposed by society had become too great. On this reading, the aim need not be stoic fortitude in the face of the inevitably tragic human condition—and we should be suspicious of such "fated" accounts—but rather political commitment to change social conditions so as to support human flourishing.[90]

We will return to that interpretation of the commonalities, as well as the differences, between Freud's views and Marx's theory of alienation in the final chapter. As an example of what Lear is suggesting, however, it is worth noting Freud's response to the October Revolution in Russia in 1917. Despite his criticisms of Marxists as being excessively optimistic about human nature and its capacity for change, he watched the early years of the Revolution with great interest, describing it as "a tremendous experiment" and went as far as to argue that:

> At a time when the great nations announce that they expect salvation only from the maintenance of Christian piety, the revolution in Russia—in spite of all its disagreeable details—seems none the less like the message of a better future.[91]

The next section of this chapter will provide a short outline of some of Freud's key ideas and point to the debates to which they have given rise. After that, I will discuss the ways in which Marxists at different times and places have sought to extract the radical kernel from Freud's thought and to integrate this into a Marxist worldview. The final part of the chapter will discuss more recent attempts to promote a political Freud, based on the writings of the French psychoanalyst Jacques Lacan and his most famous contemporary disciple Slavoj Žižek. I shall conclude by assessing what contribution, if any, psychoanalytic theory can make both to interpreting the world in which we live and also to changing it.

## Freud: the unconscious and sexuality

Since its earliest years, psychoanalysis has been a highly controversial theory; its key assertions challenged not only by critics hostile to the entire project but also by dissident colleagues or former colleagues of Freud and by later generations of psychoanalysts. In terms of what unites the many schools of psychoanalysts today (and psychoanalysis outdoes even the far left in its propensity to split into rival and competing factions) Frosh suggests two things: firstly, a shared belief that unconscious phenomena exist and secondly, a practice geared to understanding these phenomena and exploring what happens to them in the context of the live encounter between analyst and patient (or "analysand").[92]

Here two of Freud's key concepts, the unconscious and his theory of sexuality, will be considered. The fact that there are so few areas of agreement among psychoanalysts underlines the extent of disagreement over some of his most basic ideas. These include his theory of child development as a psychosexual progression through oral, anal and genital stages, each of which poses particular challenges and is resolved (successfully or otherwise) in the Oedipus complex; his theory of drives, based initially on the sexual drive and the drive for self-preservation, to which he later added a death drive; and his structural model of the mind as comprised of id (the unconscious), ego (the conscious "I") and superego (the voice of authority in the form of parent and society).

Each of these theories has been challenged or amended by successive generations of psychoanalysts (as well as being revised by Freud himself throughout his life) and some of these challenges and debates will be touched on below.

### The unconscious

As noted above, the belief that unconscious mental phenomena exist and shape our behaviour in ways which we are (by definition) normally unaware (in ourselves, if not in others) is one which is shared by all schools of psychoanalysis. As with all of his key early concepts, Freud claimed to have arrived at this belief through his experience as a clinician of listening to what his emotionally disturbed patients were saying, or more frequently not saying since it was primarily their silences, slips of the tongue, evasions, shifts in tone, body language and above all, the content of their dreams that pointed him to the existence of the unconscious:

> When I set myself the task of bringing to light what human beings keep hidden within them...I thought the task was a harder one than it really is. He that has eyes to see and ears to hear may convince himself that no mortal can keep a secret. If his lips are silent he chatters with his finger-tips; betrayal oozes out of him at every pore.[93]

The idea that our conscious behaviour is shaped by forces of which we are usually unaware has meant that Freud has often been portrayed as a crude determinist. Joel Kovel argues, however, that his portrayal of the relationship between unconscious mental activities and the conscious mind is a much more subtle and complex one than is usually suggested:

> Freud never uttered the nonsense that behaviour was simply determined by the unconscious. He held rather that it emerged out of the impact of unconscious wishes on given reality. Behaviour is formed, so to speak, at the boundary between conscious and unconscious thought (which latter registers the objective world)—a radical boundary, given the nature of repression which sees to it that the unconscious never rejoins its conscious correlate. So Freud's thought can be called "dialectical" since it is the interplay between different forms of experience rather than any one of them that determines behaviour. The unconscious is in need of special attention because under everyday circumstances it gets no attention. Psychoanalysis is therefore but a form of compensatory attention.[94]

Freud's key contribution, then, was not the discovery of an unconscious region of the mind—others had already proposed that view—but the assertion that the relationship between the unconscious and conscious mind was a *dynamic* one, based on repression. For Freud, the unconscious is the repository of repressed infantile thoughts, wishes, beliefs—repressed because they are forbidden or perceived as dangerous. Although repressed and out of conscious mind, however, they continue to make their presence felt, both in the ways described above and also through neuroses—anxieties, depressions, phobias and so on. The aim of psychoanalytic treatment is to bring such disturbing infantile beliefs and memories into consciousness in a safe setting to allow them to be addressed in an adult manner (or in Freud's much-quoted phrase, to "transform neurotic misery into common unhappiness").

As noted above, all schools of psychoanalysis subscribe to the notion of the unconscious. That said, in terms of the politics of psychoanalysis, the more conformist versions of psychoanalysis that dominated in the post-war period in the USA in particular placed much more emphasis on the ego, the "rational" part of the psyche, than on the id, which includes the unconscious dimension.[95] By contrast, the focus of more radical psychoanalytical approaches from the Frankfurt School in the 1930s to those based on the ideas of the French analyst Jacques Lacan have placed greater emphasis on the unconscious as a container of the "truth" of the ways in which capitalism, primarily through the institution of the family, represses our most basic needs and emotions.

## Sexuality

A frequent criticism of Freud, both in his own time and today, is that he "reduced everything to sex". The Canadian Marxist Susan Rosenthal, for example, has described Freud as "a charlatan" who "reduced mind to genitals".[96] As he himself observed in *An Autobiographical Study*:

> Few of the findings of psych-analysis have met with such universal contradiction or have aroused such an outburst of indignation as the assertion that the sexual function starts at the beginning of life and reveals its presence by important signs even in childhood.[97]

Nor were these expressions of indignation and outrage confined to the respectable bourgeois. In *Freudianism: a Marxist Critique*, published in Russia in 1927, the Bolshevik writer V N Voloshinov argued that the "basic ideological motif" of Freudianism was that:

> A human being's fate, the whole content of his life and creative activity—of his art, if he is an artist; of his science, if he is a scientist, of his political programs and measures, if he is a politician, and so on—are wholly and exclusively determined by his sexual instinct. Everything else represents merely the overtones of the mighty melody of sex.[98]

In addressing these criticisms, the first point to note is that Freud appears to have arrived at his view of infantile sexuality slowly and reluctantly, based on the discussions and analyses which took place in his consulting room:

[S]ince these experiences of childhood were always concerned with sexual excitations and the reaction against them, I found myself faced by the fact of infantile sexuality—once again a novelty and a contradiction of one of the strongest of human prejudices. Childhood was looked upon as "innocent" and free from the lusts of sex, and the fight with the demon of "sensuality" was not thought to begin until the troubled age of puberty. Such occasional sexual activities as it had been impossible to overlook in children were put down as signs of degeneracy or premature depravity or as a curious freak of nature.[99]

As is well known, Freud originally believed that the sexual experiences which his patients described were in each case the result of actual incest, rape or sexual abuse. His abandonment of this "seduction theory" and his revised view that such accounts were frequently based on fantasy has been the subject of huge controversy with critics, notably Jeffrey Masson, accusing Freud of hypocrisy and cowardice, of abandoning the seduction theory so as not to alienate respectable Viennese society.[100] Even close colleagues of Freud such as Sándor Ferenczi in his later years reverted to the view that in all likelihood Freud's early female patients had indeed been the victims of actual rape or abuse.

Given what is now known about the prevalence of sexual abuse (according to NSPCC figures, approximately one in 20 children experience it in some form) and given also the research evidence (to be discussed in Chapter 5) for a link between child sexual abuse and the onset of psychosis in later life, the possibility that generations of abused women (and a smaller number of men) may have been told by their analysts that the rape they claim to have experienced actually never happened should be a matter of huge concern. Given also Freud's views on issues such as the alleged superiority of the "vaginal orgasm" over the clitoral organism, it is hardly surprising that many in the early feminist movement saw him as an enemy and a key ideological contributor to women's oppression, especially given the very conformist brand of psychoanalysis which dominated American culture in the 1950s.

In response to these criticisms, Freud's defenders on the left have responded in two ways. Firstly, they argue, Freud never denied either the reality or the impact of actual childhood sexual abuse. According to Lear:

It is important to note that Freud never abandoned the idea that children were abused, and that abuse caused lasting psychological harm. What he abandoned was the idea that the stories of sexual seduction he was hearing from the couch—however sincere—were always and everywhere giving a true account of actual events.[101]

Secondly, if, as some critics have alleged, Freud's main concern in abandoning the seduction theory was to maintain his own respectability, then he went about it in a decidedly odd way. For following the abandonment of the seduction theory, sexuality occupied a *more*, not a *less*, central place in his account of human development and pathology:

> Abandoning the seduction theory presented Freud with a significant intellectual opportunity. He was able to expand his account of what was sexual. For if some of his patients were giving vivid accounts of sexual encounters that, in fact, never occurred, it gave him reason to think that sex was alive in the imagination in ways that needed to be explored and understood. The imagination seemed able to endow a person with a sexual life even though the person had no sexual life—at least as ordinarily understood.[102]

Similarly Frosh notes, "the abandonment of the seduction theory was the founding moment for psychoanalysis itself. Because it introduced the idea that patients' *fantasies* might be the key element in their psychopathology".[103]

The point is an important one. It means that far from reducing human behaviour to animal or biological instincts (although he never denied the biological basis of the sexual drive), what Freud is proposing is something very different: in the words of the Marxist feminist Juliet Mitchell, a *humanised* theory of sexuality, central to which is the human capacity for imagination.[104] As Lear argues, for Freud our sexuality is a model for what makes us human. It is no coincidence that in his *Three Essays on Sexuality* (first published in 1905) he begins with a discussion of fetishes and argues that "no other variation of the sexual drive can lay so much claim to our interest as this one". Why? Because what fetishes demonstrate is that in humans, unlike animals, there is no necessary connection between the sexual object (the person or thing to which we feel sexual attraction) and the sexual *aim* (the act towards which the drive tends). As Lear puts it:

Think of it this way: a bird may happen to build a nest in a lady's shoe. And, in building the nest, the bird may show a heightened concern for the shoe. But the bird cannot thereby make the shoe into a fetish. Why not? Is it lack of imagination on the bird's part? In an important sense the answer to this question is "yes"... Unlike other animals, human sexuality is *essentially* imaginative—that is, essentially open to imaginative variability. One consequence is that all sorts of activities are going to count as sexual that have no relation to reproduction; another consequence is that when humans finally do get round to reproducing, they are going to reproduce imaginative animals.[105]

One is reminded here of Marx's comments regarding the difference between "human nature" and "animal nature" and the huge scope for human imagination:

A spider conducts operations that resemble those of a weaver, and a bee puts to shame many an architect in the construction of her cells. But what distinguishes the worst architect from the best of bees is this, that the architect raises his structure in imagination before he erects it in reality.[106]

Not surprisingly then, Freud had a much less fixed view of what constituted "normal sexuality" than most of his contemporaries and was a fierce critics of those "zealots" who sought to repress every "deviation" from what they considered normal, especially homosexuality. Writing in 1905 he argued:

We must learn to speak without indignation of what we call the sexual perversions—instances in which the sexual function has extended its limits in respect either to the part of the body concerned or to the sexual object chosen. The uncertainty in regard to the boundaries of what is to be called normal sexual life, when we take different races and different epochs into account, should in itself be enough to cool the zealot's ardour.[107]

That view of sexuality as fluid, with bisexuality the norm rather than an aberration, led some leading feminists in the 1970s, such as Juliet Mitchell in the UK and Phylis Chesler in the USA, to see psychoanalytic thinking "which posited a dynamic reality and no gendered essentials" not as intrinsically oppressive but instead as "women's best hope for escaping a reduction to essentialist terms".[108]

Similarly, a small number of American psychoanalysts in the 1970s were able to go back to Freud's 1905 views as a basis for their support of the gay movement's campaign to remove homosexuality from the DSM where it was classified as a mental illness. Since then, as Herzog notes, there has been a dramatic turnaround in psychoanalysts' attitudes towards homosexuality:

> Already the 1990s saw countless workshops, committees, initiatives, conference papers and publications—even journal launchings that showed how eager the analytic community was to renew itself by learning from gays and lesbians. In addition, more more openly gay and lesbian individuals became analysts.[109]

That turnaround in attitudes and professional practice was clearly welcome. It should not of course be allowed to obscure the "horrible history" of conformist psychoanalysis over several previous decades of oppression of LGBT individuals.

What that history also shows, however, is that psychoanalytic ideas, in common with other worldviews such as Christianity or Islam, do not exist in a social and political vacuum. They are shaped by the wider social, political and ideological context in which they operate so, not surprisingly, the main traditions in psychoanalysis—individualist and conformist—have usually mirrored the dominant ideas in society more generally.

What is also true, however, is that especially in periods of social change and upheaval, more radical understandings of these ideas can come to the fore. It was not an accident, for example, that the American Psychiatric Association abandoned its classification of homosexuality as a mental illness in 1973. Rather, it was due to the rise in the preceding years of a vocal and assertive gay rights movement which successfully challenged the Association's designation of their sexuality as pathological. Nor was this an isolated example. In the next part of the chapter we will look at other examples of sections of the radical left seeking to deploy psychoanalytic ideas as part of the struggle against oppression and exploitation.

## Freud and the Bolsheviks

As well as resulting in sweeping political and economic change, the 1917 October Revolution in Russia saw a massive outpouring of intellectual, creative and artistic energy. Every area of life and culture was transformed, even in the face of the enormous hardship and suffering caused by the subsequent civil war. Describing the situation in 1919, Victor Serge wrote:

> Despite this immense poverty, a tremendous impulse was given to popular education. Such a thirst for knowledge was revealed in the country that new schools, adult courses, universities and workers' colleges sprung up everywhere. Innumerable experiments discovered new and hitherto unexplored fields. Schools for backward children were founded; a whole system of kindergartens sprung up; and abbreviated adult courses put education within the reach of workers for the first time. The conquest of the universities began somewhat later.[110]

It was against this background of a widespread openness to, and enthusiasm for, new ways of thinking and living that the ideas of psychoanalysis began to make their presence felt in the young Soviet Union. According to American academic Martin Miller in his study of this period:

> For a time...it seemed as if psychoanalysis might be able to play an important role in shaping the new postrevolutionary order. This hope rested on the possibility of making some acceptable contribution to the creation of a Marxist psychology, one of the projects called for by the Communist Party during the early 1920s.[111]

Nor was this an idle hope. The first post-revolutionary lecture course on psychoanalysis was given during the winter of 1919-1920 by Dr Tatania Rosenthal, chief physician at the Institute for Brain Pathology in Petrograd and according to Miller "a Social Democrat who had greeted the revolution with enthusiasm". Rosenthal put her ideas into practice by setting up a school for children with emotional problems and learning disabilities based on psychoanalytic principles.

Psychoanalysis appears to have flourished in the early years of the Revolution, attracting the support and active involvement of leading Marxist psychologists such as Lev Vygotsky and A R Luria (the latter a major intellectual influence on the late British neurologist Oliver Sacks, who was also an adherent of psychoanalysis). In part this was for theoretical reasons. In a memoir, Luria recalled his own excitement at encountering Freud's early writings:

Here, I thought, was a scientific approach that combined a strongly deterministic explanation of concrete, individual behaviour with an explanation of the origins of complex human needs in terms of natural science.[112]

A more immediate reason for the interest was the fact that the civil war had resulted in large numbers of orphaned children who needed to be cared for and psychoanalysts were active in setting up new forms of residential childcare provision.

Support for psychoanalysis was not, moreover, confined to a few progressive psychologists. As Miller argues, it would have been difficult for the Moscow Psychoanalytic Institute to have functioned so visibly without support from the Bolshevik Party. The fact that Freud's works were being published by the state publishing house shows that some key party leaders, most notably Trotsky but also allegedly Nikolai Bukharin, Karl Radek and Adolf Ioffe, were favourably disposed towards psychoanalysis.

Summing up this period, Miller concludes that the years 1921-1923 "were the high tide of the psychoanalytic movement in Russia":

[P]sychoanalysis achieved spectacular successes at this time. An institute with a fully recognised training programme was inaugurated, an outpatient clinic was established together with the children's home, all functioning on psychoanalytic principles. The extensive publication of psychoanalytic books and articles was proceeding at a level that was difficult to imagine a few years before. All of these activities were in some measure supported by the state. Indeed it can safely be said (with all the implied ironies, given what was to come later) that no government was ever responsible for supporting psychoanalysis to such an extent, before or after.[113]

That did not mean, of course, that a majority of psychologists, let alone a majority of party leaders, supported psychoanalysis (though Miller hints that Lenin may have been less hostile than has sometimes been suggested). The key point, however, is that the debates which took place during this period over the status of psychoanalysis and the extent to which it was a materialist science were *real* debates, conducted in an atmosphere of openness and genuine enquiry. With the rise of the Stalinist bureaucracy from the mid-1920s onwards and the rigid imposition of a Party line in psychology as in every other area of life, that was no longer the case. As Andrew Collier argues:

> The great downturn in the prospects of co-operation [between Marxism and psychoanalysis] came with Stalin. The suppression of psychoanalysis in Russia was part of the same puritanical programme which led to prison sentences for homosexuals, the prohibition of abortion, the preaching of sexual abstinence to students, the awarding of state prizes to particularly prolific mothers, and so on.[114]

### Germany: the lost revolution

The Russian Revolution was part of a great revolutionary wave which swept across Europe between 1917 and 1923 and which led to revolutionary upheavals in several other countries including Hungary, Italy and Germany. In these countries too there was an openness to Freud's ideas on the left during this period and much debate and discussion about the extent to which they were compatible with a Marxist worldview. As an example, in 1919 under the short-lived Hungarian Soviet Republic, Freud's close colleague Sándor Ferenczi was granted a professorship and a department of psychoanalysis was established within the Budapest University's faculty of medicine. This was the first time that psychoanalysis had ever been fully integrated into a medical curriculum.

In his study of the German analyst Otto Fenichel and the "political Freudians", Russell Jacoby gives some sense of the degree of psychoanalytic interest in Marxist ideas (and vice versa) at this time:

> Today it is easy to forget how many early psychoanalysts identified themselves as socialists and Marxists. They may even have constituted a majority. They included Paul Federn, Helene Deutsch, Siegfried Bernfeld, Herma Nunberg, Annie and Wilhelm Reich, Edith Jacobson, Willi Hoffer, Martin Grotjahn, Karl Landauer, Bruno Bettleheim, Ernst Simmel and Fenichel. Before the onset of fascism these were not isolated individuals. Located in Vienna and Berlin in the politically charged atmosphere of the late 1920s and early 1930s, their lives and projects frequently over-lapped.[115]

Jacoby also points to the large number of women who were part of the psychoanalytic movement at this time and argues that:

Regardless of the relative accuracy (or inaccuracy) of Freud's theory of female sexuality, indisputably psychoanalysis breathed of a sexual enlightenment and emancipation especially germane to women; psychoanalysis viewed women as sexual beings. Freud left no doubt that his female patients—originally the bulk of his practice—suffered from repression, sexual ignorance and misinformation.[116]

It was a movement which did not survive the rise of Nazism. Many of its adherents who did not perish in Hitler's death camps (and there was a high representation of Jews in the early psychoanalytic movement) fled to the USA, where their status as refugees meant they were forced to conceal their political views, especially during the period of the Cold War. As Jacoby shows, psychoanalysts such as Otto Fenichel and his circle never ceased to consider themselves Marxists and maintained secret communication and political discussion for decades but chose not to go public with their ideas.

Other émigrés to the USA such as Wilhelm Reich, who had been a leading figure within the psychoanalytic movement in the late 1920s during which time he made a serious attempt to achieve an integration of Marxism and psychoanalysis, moved in the 1930s and 1940s towards an extreme biologism. As Kovel argues, the roots of that biologism lay in Reich's particular interpretation of Freud's theory of sexuality:

> From his earliest days in psychoanalysis, he felt that actual experience, and notably sexual experience, remained the touchstone. While he continued to do important psychological work for a number of years, one senses that for Reich, mind—the whole congeries of fantasy and thought, wish and desire—was always epiphenomenal to the reality of the functioning body. By the mid-twenties he had already taken Freud's original ideas about sexual release to the point of specifying the orgasm as the criteria of healthy functioning. At the same time, he was developing his ideas about character into a form that would later take shape, first as "muscular armour", and eventually as a transducer of universal biological energy, the *orgone*.[117]

Expelled from the psychoanalytic movement for being too Marxist and from the Communist Party for being too psychoanalytic, Reich moved away from both worldviews, with his therapeutic practice increasingly focused on the body, sometimes in rather bizarre ways. He died in a US penitentiary in 1957 having being convicted of fraudulently promoting an "orgone box" which he claimed could measure the patient's universal energy levels.

Reich is now largely written out of the history of psychoanalysis, barely meriting a footnote in most texts. Yet while his ideas undoubtedly became increasingly wacky (to the extent that it is often suggested he suffered from a mental illness in his later years), the work from his Marxist period in the late 1920s and early 1930s, including his analysis of the mass psychology of fascism, repays study, while his emphasis on the relationship between sexual repression and ruling class domination, if over-stated, remains valid.

In part, Reich's single-minded stress on the sexual instinct was a reaction against what he saw as the increasingly conformist direction in which psychoanalysis was moving in the 1930s. That conformism was significantly reinforced by the relocation of psychoanalysis to the USA following the rise of fascism in Europe in the 1930s. The political climate there was far from conducive to radical ideas, especially in the post-war McCarthy period and even more so for German-speaking refugees. Furthermore, and against Freud's express wishes, the American Psychoanalytic Association required that all practising psychoanalysts should also be medical doctors. The result was a psychoanalysis concerned not with the wild and unruly desires of the id nor with the workings of an explosive and disruptive sexual drive but rather an ego psychology whose main concern was with helping patients to adjust to "reality", the reality of a post-war America.[118]

## Jacques Lacan: France's psychoanalytic revolution

The failure of the German Revolution of 1919-1923 in the face of apparently favourable objective conditions led some on the left to conclude that what Marxism lacked was a "theory of subjectivity", a theoretical framework which could make sense of the complex interaction between these wider objective conditions and working class consciousness. Marxists such as Wilhelm Reich and Erich Fromm looked for that framework in the ideas of psychoanalysis.

The experience of the "May events" in France some 50 years later led some to a similar conclusion but in this case to the version of psychoanalysis developed by the leading French analyst Jacques Lacan. According to one historian of France's "psychoanalytic politics":

> For a short while the May events looked like a revolution in the making but then suddenly they were over. After the events, people were left hungry for a way to continue to think about sexuality and self-expression as part of a revolutionary movement, for a way to think about the personal as the political and social. "Thinking through the events" required a theory that integrated society and the individual. Lacan provided that theory in his ideas about the transition from the imaginary to symbolic realm, the transition from presocial to social with the acquisition of language.[119]

Before discussing the extent to which Lacan's ideas can provide the theory of subjectivity allegedly missing from Marxism, it is worth noting the strong similarities between the Second International Marxism against which Korsch, Fromm and the Frankfurt School were rebelling in the 1920s and 1930s and the Stalinised version of Marxism promoted by the post-war communist parties, including the French Communist Party (PCF). John Molyneux, in a paper on the "real Marxist tradition" describes the latter as a "carbon copy" of the former.[120] Given, then, both the theoretical bankruptcy of the PCF and the thoroughly reactionary role it played during the May Events (typified by the dismissal by its leadership of the young student revolutionaries as "the sons of the rich bourgeois...who will quickly turn off their revolutionary ardour and go back to managing Daddy's firm"), [121] it is hardly surprising that many of those involved should have looked for political and theoretical alternatives outside "official" Marxism to make sense of their experience.

Also worth noting is the fact that, as in the 1920s, the interest in psychoanalytic ideas in France (a country which until then had been mainly resistant to these ideas) followed on the heels of the defeat of a revolutionary, or near revolutionary, moment. In that respect, as Turkle notes, there were similarities between the experience in France following the May events and developments in the USA:

> The fact that a group of French activist students of the troubled late 1960s searched for personal solutions when a political solution seemed to have failed might not seem surprising. After all, a similar phenomenon swept

American campuses in the early 1970s as energies once spent on radical politics were redirected into encounter groups, religious cults and the human potential movement. France and America have much in common. In both countries, political disillusionment was followed by an outburst of interest in transformation of the spirit and the psyche.[122]

That said, and as she notes, the interest in Lacanian psychoanalysis in France did not necessarily signal a move away from political involvement but rather involved an attempt to deepen political understanding and to provide a fuller explanation of the May events and their aftermath. It was a period when "French psychoanalysis became more permeable to politics and politics more permeable to it".[123]

Lacan's ideas, as has often been noted, are notoriously difficult, even obscure. The kindest explanation for this is that on the one hand, his particular version of psychoanalysis was highly theoretical and drew on several different philosophical traditions—principally phenomenology, structural anthropology, linguistic theory and the writings of Hegel— and on the other, Lacan was first and foremost a clinician for whom speech and language were the very substance of psychoanalysis. For that reason, he believed that speech, specifically the weekly public seminars which he held from the 1950s onwards and which became enormously popular and influential, was a more effective way of conveying the experience of what was going on between analyst and patient than the written text. To complicate things even further, his ideas, like those of Freud, changed throughout his lifetime so when reading Lacan, it is important to place these ideas in their specific context.

There is a huge volume of literature on Lacan's ideas and their applications, both from within the world of psychoanalysis and even more so from the field of literary and cultural studies. Much of the recent interest in these ideas in the English-speaking world has been stimulated by the writings of the philosopher Slavoj Žižek, dubbed by Terry Eagleton "Lacan's representative on earth". Here it is possible only to give the briefest outline of these ideas.

A useful starting point is to consider who and what Lacan was arguing against. The dominant psychoanalytic school in the USA in the early 1950s, when Lacan began his seminars, was based on what was known as "ego psychology", centred on a group of New York analysts whose leading members included German émigré Heinz Hartmann and Lacan's own one-time analyst, Rudolf Lowenstein. Daniel Pick describes this school of thought as follows:

> While these analysts did much to consolidate the status of the talking cure, this achievement came at a price. Certainly many, including Lacan, balked at their vision of analysis facilitating a "healthy" ego's optimal adaptation, fine-tuned to test reality, albeit allowing some margin for individual compulsions, idiosyncracies and passions. Lacan saw ego psychology as itself an adaptation of Freud's ideas to an individualistic, optimistic society, replete with rose-tinted dreams.[124]

Against this view of the role of psychoanalysis as being to cultivate a smoothly functioning integrated ego, adapted to the realities of post-war consumerist capitalism, Lacan advocated a "return to Freud", a rediscovery of the real radicalism of Freud's theory which challenged both the ego-psychologists' dominant notion of the relationship between the ego and the unconscious (or id) and more generally, their view of the role of analysis. He did so on the basis of a new set of categories, or more accurately orders of experience, which he called the *Imaginary*, the *Symbolic* and the *Real*.

The starting point for understanding the Imaginary is the experience of the small child. As Eagleton argues, for Freud:

> The small infant is in the grip of an anarchic set of bodily drives from which the ego is yet to emerge. When it does appear on the scene it represses a good many of the forces which went into its making, thrusting them into that non-place we know as the unconscious.[125]

This emergence of the ego, Lacan argued in a famous early paper on "the mirror stage", comes as a result of the child seeking to overcome his terrifying sense of fragmentation and achieving an imaginary unity through seeing his own image reflected back to him, whether literally in a mirror or in the responses and faces of his caregivers. Frosh explains Lacan's thesis as follows:

> The idea is that the fragmentary infant catches a glimpse of itself in the mirror (the actual mirror or the "mirror" of the mother's gaze) and identifies with this image, leaping with relief into the fantasy that because it can see itself as an entire *physical* being, it is also a whole *psychological* subject... This is taken by Lacan as the origin of the ego. In

opposition to those who see ego development as the main way in which an infant progresses to stability and authenticity, Lacan claims that the ego is adopted as a kind of defence, an armour or shell supporting the psyche, which is otherwise experienced as in fragments.

In adult life (and for Lacan, these are not simply stages of development but orders of experience which we carry with us throughout our lives), the dominance of the Imaginary leads to the fantasy that we can find "wholeness" and "authenticity", either in our friendships with other people or through therapy. In that sense, as Eagleton comments, "imaginary is, in short, a kind of ideology" (an idea which formed the basis for a famous paper by Louis Althusser).

The basis of the Imaginary is the child's fantasy that it is possible to have total fusion with another, usually the mother. The realisation that there is a world out there which disrupts that blissful union of mother and child—what Lacan calls the Other—comes in the form of *language*:

> Lacanians see language as a structure that pre-exists the individual "subject". This means it operates as a kind of regulatory *law*, making some things easy and other things difficult. The need to use language therefore interferes with the Imaginary fantasy, revealing that the relationship with the other is already organised by something outside it. This realisation on the part of the infant is the moment at which she or he enters the Symbolic order.[126]

Without entering the Symbolic Order, the child could not cope with his or her social environment. Nevertheless, as Frosh suggests, "giving up the fantasy of one-ness is painful and never fully accomplished, as Imaginary experience is central to much of human consciousness".[127] It persists for example in the notion of romantic love, central to which is the feeling that at last you have met someone who completely understands you and in whom you can find—and lose—yourself. As both small child and smitten lover discover, however, this is a difficult fantasy to sustain and one which frequently ends in disappointment!

While space does not permit a fuller discussion, it is important to note that the Symbolic is also Lacan's version of Freud's Oedipus Complex in which the (male) child gives up (in fantasy) his claim on the mother on pain of castration by the father—thus the Symbolic

Order involves both language and sexuality. Less dramatically, Terry Eagleton suggests that "the passage from the imaginary to the symbolic is one from the closed sphere of the ego and its objects to the open field of intersubjectivity".[128] It is the child's entry into "culture". Žižek describes the Symbolic Order in this way:

> When we speak (or listen, for that matter) we never merely interact with others; our speech activity is grounded in our accepting and relying on a complex network of rules and other kinds of presuppositions. First there are the grammatical rules that we have to master blindly and spontaneously: if I were to bear these rules in mind all the time, my speech would break down. Then there is the background of participating in the same life-world that enables me and my partner to understand each other. The rules that I follow are marked by a deep divide: there are rules (and meanings) that I follow blindly, out of habit, but of which, if I reflect, I can become at least partially aware (such as common grammatical rules); and there are rules that I follow, meanings that haunt me, in ignorance (such as unconscious prohibitions). Then there are rules and meanings I know of, but must not be seen to know of—dirty or obscene innuendos that one passes over in silence in order to keep up the proper appearances.

As he adds, "The symbolic space acts like a yardstick against which I can measure myself".

The Real, the third element of Lacan's trilogy, is, as Terry Eagleton notes, "an enigmatic concept". Similarly, Žižek, quoting Lacan, argues that:

> [T]he Lacanian Real is a much more complex category than the idea of a fixed transhistorical "hard core" that forever eludes symbolisation: it has nothing to do with what the German Idealist Immanuel Kant called the "Thing-in-Itself", reality the way it is out there, independently of us, prior to being skewed by our perceptions."… this notion is not at all Kantian. I even insist on this. If there is a notion of the real, it is extremely complex and incomprehensible, it cannot be comprehended in a way that would make an All out of it.[129]

Frosh suggests it is:

> That which precedes the various splits or moments of alienation enacted through the imaginary and the symbolic. The Real is not a mystical

order outside the realm of experience; rather it is what our psychological and social devices keep at bay. At certain times it breaks through to link us with everything we have left out. But much of the time it pulses away as a threat, as that which can demolish all our attempts at self-identity.[130]

Not surprisingly, then, as Eagleton argues, it is above all in dreams rather than in that "set of shop-soiled fictions we know as reality" that we approach "the Real of our desire":

> The Real is what disrupts these agreeable fabrications, skewing the subject out of shape and bending the symbolic order out of true. It is the subject's point of failure and impasse, the way it fails to be at one with itself, the primordial wound we incurred by our expulsion from the pre-Oedipal Eden. It is the gash in our being where we were torn loose from the maternal body, and from which desire flows unstaunchably.[131]

Slightly more prosaically, Eagleton suggests, it is what the author Milan Kundera has called the "theme" of an individual's identity—the "truth" of a person in the sense of their unique experiences of desire and loss.

What are we to make of all this? The first thing to note is that Lacan's ideas have been extremely influential within the psychoanalytic profession, mainly in France but not only there: according to Frosh around 50 percent of British psychoanalysts would now see themselves as working within a Lacanian framework. It may be that these ideas are helpful to analysts working with their patients' fantasies and symbolic relationships. Whether, however, they are of value to Marxists seeking to change the world (and to be fair, Lacan himself never made any such claim for his ideas) is more doubtful. In an insightful assessment of Lacan in *International Socialism* in 1980, Andrew Collier pointed to an important difference between the theories of Freud and those of Lacan:

> If we look at Freud's account of character-formation, we find children internalising the family as a result of relations of love, envy identification and so on towards their parents and siblings. The child's conception of its family will not be altogether realistic, as it will be affected by wishful and fearful phantasies; but the starting point of the child's development is its real human environment... One gets a very different impression from Lacan. We no longer hear much about

fathers but a great deal about the Name-of-the-Father, the Law of the Father and so on. These notions seem to be independent of particular family structures.[132]

While Freud's theories, then, are thoroughly materialist—as Collier says, for Freud "real biological needs and real social relations precede and ultimately determine material life (whether conscious or unconscious)"—the same cannot be said for those of Lacan. And his version of idealism poses not only theoretical problems; it also creates major political and strategic challenges for those who wish to deploy those ideas to bring about social change. Responding, for example, to Juliet Mitchell's Lacanian argument that "It is the specific feature of patriarchy—the law of the hypothesised pre-historic murdered father—that defines the relative places of men and women in human history", Collier wryly observes:

> It is one thing to fight for women's equality, gay rights, abortion on demand, and communal nurseries. But if the principal enemy is a long-dead ancestor who never in fact existed, we are going to need a new strategy altogether. Perhaps the answer is to restore the Nibelung's ring to the Rhinemaidens.[133]

## Concluding comments

Alex Callinicos usefully summarises three ways in which Freud can be seen to have contributed to the development of social theory and by extension, to our understanding of mental health and mental distress.

Firstly, "the distinction between normality and abnormality...is relativised. Repression is a universal phenomenon, at work in the healthy and the ill alike". Mental health and mental distress, in other words, are not discrete categories but rather points on a spectrum: we are all more or less neurotic (or psychotic).

Secondly, "gender differences are not simply the result of the biological constitution of male and female human beings—or rather, the effects of this constitution are mediated by the process through which, within male-dominated family structures, girls and boys are prepared for their future roles within these same structures."

Thirdly, "the conscious self turns out to be the result of a history, a complex assemblage of desires and dispositions whose internal tensions both conceal and allude to a vast, unknown hinterland in which many of the most important effects of the process through which it was constructed lie hidden".[134]

In short then, in an age where cognitive-behavioural therapies in particular are often used as a means of securing rapid behavioural change and even for coercing people back into the workforce, a strength of psychoanalysis is that it recognises the complexities of people's motives and desires and that the "symptoms" which we display often have a meaning which we should seek to understand rather than simply repress or eliminate. As one recent sympathetic account argues:

> Twenty-first-century pharmaceutical and neuroscentific research— often bent on ignoring social context and interpersonal relations and intent on refiguring selfhood as a matter mostly of chemical reactions and/or encoding in the genes—has had very little to say, for example, about such crucial features of human existence as conflicting desires, the instabilities of meanings, of the ever-mysterious relationships between social contexts and psychic interiority and social context. Psychoanalysis, in all its contradictions, absurdities and self-revisions, can contribute a great deal on precisely these matters.[135]

At best, then, psychoanalysis, and therapies informed by psychoanalysis, can provide those experiencing persistent emotional difficulties with a safe space, a trusting relationship and the conceptual tools to make sense of patterns of thinking, feeling and behaving (often rooted in early life experience) which are causing them distress. That is not an unimportant contribution and we should insist that such therapies be made available on the NHS, as opposed to reliance on a "one size fits all" CBT approach.

Where psychoanalysis has less to contribute, however, is in the explanation of wider social and economic phenomena or historical events. Where it does attempt such explanations, not only is the result usually highly speculative (as for example in Freud's own later works such as *Civilisation and its Discontents*) but it also often involves substituting essentialist, static concepts, such as poor parenting or innate drives, for a detailed empirical analysis of the totality of factors—economic, social, state of the class struggle and so on—contributing to current levels of consciousness in society.

The same criticism can be levelled at the concept of social character, developed by Erich Fromm. By social character, Fromm was referring to the ways in which capitalism seeks to create particular character types (for example, the "authoritarian character" or the "consumerist character") to ensure the smooth functioning of the system. The concept is clearly not without value. Under neoliberal capitalism, for example, it is not difficult to see the ways in which individuals are encouraged, or even coerced, into seeing themselves as wholly responsible for every aspect of their lives, including their health. As one writer has observed:

> Health becomes an individual goal, a social and moral responsibility, and a site for routine biomedical intervention...the focus is no longer on illness, disability and disease as matters of fate, but on health as a matter of ongoing moral transformation.[136]

So the creation of a particular kind of psychology or social character is one way in which the ruling class seeks to ensure compliance with its rule. The danger, however, is in over-estimating either its success in doing so—as Antonio Gramsci observed, working class consciousness is always full of contradictions[137]—or the relative significance of individual psychology vis-à-vis a whole range of more important factors such as the state of the economy, the level of class struggle, the weight of political parties and so on. As I have argued elsewhere, whatever the merits of Fromm's concept, it risks reifying working class consciousness, of seeing it as fixed or static, and becoming a substitute for a concrete analysis of the factors shaping people's thoughts and feelings.[138]

# 4

# "Mad to be normal": the politics of anti-psychiatry

IN July 1967 an extraordinary conference took place at the Roundhouse in London. Entitled "The Dialectics of Liberation", its aims were "to demystify human violence in all its forms, the social systems from which it emanates, and to explore new forms of action". What made the conference historic, however, was not so much the extent to which it met—or perhaps not surprisingly, failed to meet—these grand aims but rather that it brought together in one place several of the leading luminaries of the 1960s' New Left. These included Black Panthers' leader Stokely Carmichael; Frankfurt School philosopher and New Left guru Herbert Marcuse; John Gerassi, friend and comrade of both Jean-Paul Sartre and Che Guevara; the Beat poet Alan Ginsberg; the Marxist economist Paul Sweezy; and the radical psychiatrists R D Laing and David Cooper.[139]

The fact that two psychiatrists not only participated in such a subversive gathering but were in fact its principal organisers may seem odd. It was, however, a reflection of the fact that, as in post-revolutionary Russia and 1920s Weimar Germany, the social struggles of the 1960s also led to a questioning of the whole spectrum of dominant ideas, including ideas about the nature of mental health and mental illness. As Peter Sedgwick, a leading chronicler of radical movements in psychiatry in this period, explained:

> Mental illness became an urgent source of welfare politics, but at the same time touched on deeper, more intimate political structures: the relations of authority between doctor and patient, between administration and clientele, between woman and man became open to fresh and simultaneous collisions in the post-war boom years, even as the authority relations between employer and worker became continually and centrally challenged in the politics of the factory. The sixties, in most

countries of the West, constituted the high-water mark in the assertiveness of the various discontented classes.[140]

As Sedgwick observed, the movement that became known as "antipsychiatry" (a label, incidentally, invented by Cooper but rejected by most of the other leading protagonists) was the product of several diffuse and often contradictory currents. One of the earliest critics of the asylum system, for example, came not from the left but from the libertarian Tory right. In a speech to the National Institute for Mental Health in 1961, Enoch Powell, then Minister of Health, called for "nothing less than the elimination of by far the greater part of this country's mental hospitals as they exist today":

> There they stand, isolated, majestic, imperious, brooded over by the gigantic water-tower and chimney combined, rising unmistakable and daunting out of the countryside—the asylums which our forefathers built with such immense solidity to express the notions of their day.[141]

Similarly, Thomas Szasz, author of *The Myth of Mental Illness* and along with R D Laing probably the best-known "anti-psychiatrist", was a right wing libertarian who opposed all forms of state provision of mental health services and argued in favour of contractually based (that is, fee-paying) individual therapies. More generally, as Sedgwick argued in his 1982 book *Psychopolitics* (on which more later), for all the insights that thinkers such as Szasz, Laing, the sociologist Erving Goffman and the political philosopher Michel Foucault provided into the oppressive nature of official psychiatry, there were real theoretical and political limitations both to their critiques and the extent to which they offered meaningful alternatives to current forms of mental health provision.

That said, for a period in the late 1960s and early 1970s their ideas, above all those of Laing, seized the imagination of a generation of young people who saw the struggle against oppressive psychiatric systems and narrow conceptions of what was "normal" as part of the wider struggle against capitalism. In contrast, the impact of such ideas on these systems and on the actual practice of psychiatry was much more limited and by the end of the 1970s any challenge which they posed had been effectively defused and buried by an increasingly powerful biomedical psychiatry.

Some five decades on, a combination of the crisis in mental health discussed in Chapter 1, a powerful evidence-based critique of biomedical psychiatry coming from critical psychologists and psychiatrists, and the growth of a mental health service users' (or survivors') movement has led to a renewed interest in the ideas of anti-psychiatry. Recent examples of that interest include an excellent new biography of the Italian radical psychiatrist Franco Basaglia by the journalist and writer John Foot, a 2017 biopic of R D Laing called *Mad to be Normal* with the actor David Tennant playing Laing, and a well-attended conference at Liverpool Hope University in 2016 devoted to discussion of the ideas of Laing's most important critic from the left, Peter Sedgwick.

The first part of this chapter will provide an outline of Laing's key ideas as they developed through the 1960s and 1970s. Next, I will discuss the critique of Laing put forward by Sedgwick, who was also a leading figure in the post-1956 New Left in the UK, translator of the works of Victor Serge and for many years an active member of the International Socialists, the predecessor of the Socialist Workers Party (UK). Sedgwick's own ideas on mental health have gained a new following in recent years, reflected both in the conference referred to above and also in the re-publication in 2015 of *Psychopolitics*. The final part of the chapter will assess the strengths and weaknesses of Sedgwick's critique of Laing and the extent to which his own ideas contribute to a deeper critical understanding of mental health and mental distress. The relationship between the ideas of Laing and his associates and the more recent development of Mad Studies will be addressed in the next chapter.

### *The Divided Self*

Ronald David Laing was born into a working class household in the Govanhill area of Glasgow in 1927. He discussed his early life experiences and upbringing in considerable detail both in an autobiography, *Wisdom, Madness and Folly*, and in lengthy interviews with the writer Bob Mullan, later published as *Mad to be Normal* (also the title of the 2017 biopic referred to above). While the particular circumstances of his childhood and adolescence were clearly significant in terms of his later development (not many Govanhill children attended the state-aided "independent" Hutcheson Grammar School, for example), here the focus will be on his ideas and activities from the time when he became a psychiatrist in the 1950s.

Laing's first book, *The Divided Self*, was published in 1960 and was based on his earlier experiences of working as a young psychiatrist firstly in the army (this was the period of National Service) and then in Glasgow psychiatric hospitals between 1953 and 1955. In *Mad to be Normal*, he gives a flavour of the treatments on offer within psychiatric hospitals as he found them at this time:

> [I]nsulin coma was the standard practice everywhere with electric shocks sometimes being give in the middle of the coma. In the army and at Gartnavel [Royal Hospital] there was the usual range of treatment from the pre-tranquillisers of paraldehyde and barbiturates and bromides to electric shocks and insulin and lobotomy... One of the consultants at Killearn [army hospital] went round to Gartnavel once a week and did a lobotomy. I was revolted by this practice on sheer clinical grounds, and with the utter casualness with which it was done...[142]

As Laing makes clear, he was not alone in questioning the use of these new physical "treatments" in this period. Some older psychiatrists also refused to perform lobotomies or administer ECT, while elsewhere in Scotland the social psychiatrist Maxwell Jones was developing the therapeutic community approach to working with people with mental health problems. Laing's approach, as exemplified in *The Divided Self*, however, was distinctive in two respects.

Firstly, his emphasis on the "intelligibility" of severe mental illness, including schizophrenia: rather than seeing the speech and behaviour of those labelled mentally ill as meaningless babble and random antics, the output of disordered brains, he argued that these behaviours could often be understood as a more or less rational response to current or past circumstances, usually involving intolerable family pressures and demands. That view also informed Laing's practice during this period. He showed great solidarity with those labelled schizophrenic. He would on occasion, for example, spend time alone with patients held in padded cells, listening to and seeking to communicate with them.

Part of the power of *The Divided Self*, then and now, lay in Laing's ability to provide explanations of the ways in which seemingly meaningless psychotic behaviour could often be more rational than it appeared. So for example, he cites a classic psychiatric case study in which the apparently mad words and behaviour of a young male patient were presented to a lecture room of medical students by the founding father of modern psychiatry, Emil Kraepelin, as an example of catatonic excitement. In a radical re-interpretation of the case study, Laing convincingly argues that the young man's behaviour could also be seen as representing resistance to being "exhibited" by Kraepelin in this way:

> Now it seems clear that this patient's behaviour can be seen in a least two ways… One may see his behaviour as "signs" of a disease; one may see his behaviour as expressive of his existence. The existential-phenomenological construction is an inference of how the other is feeling and acting. What is the boy's experience of Kraepelin? He seems to be tormented and desperate. What is he "about" in speaking and acting in this way? He is objecting to being measured and tested. He wants to be heard.[143]

The reference to existentialism highlights the second distinguishing feature of *The Divided Self*: namely, its ambitious theoretical framework, highly unusual in the British psychiatry of the 1950s. From his late teens onwards, Laing immersed himself in philosophy and social theory, including Marx's early writings and also *Capital*. His main influences, however, were the European philosophies of phenomenology and existentialism, particularly the writings of Kierkegaard, Nietzsche and Sartre. In addition, he spent the four years prior to the publication of *The Divided Self* undergoing psychoanalytic training at the Tavistock Institute in London, steeped in the ideas of Freud and his successors. Laing's use of existentialism to make sense of schizophrenia meant that, in Peter Sedgwick's words:

> One of the most difficult of philosophies was brought to bear on one of the most baffling of mental health conditions, in a manner which, somewhat surprisingly, helped to elucidate both. Existential philosophy, with its reputation of introverted cloudiness and speculative indiscipline, was here set working in a concrete, practical and socially urgent context—the understanding of the mentally ill. Conversely, a major form of psychosis was elucidated as a mental system possessing lawful shape and sequence, comprehensible in existential terms as the outcome of rational strategies adopted by the patient in the face of an ambiguous and threatening personal environment.[144]

The extent to which Laing was successful in integrating these different philosophical traditions into a coherent worldview is a different question. And in fact one explanation for Laing's later extraordinary appeal to young people in particular was that he appeared able to espouse wildly different philosophies—Marxism, Buddhism, existentialism—at the same time, thus allowing him to be claimed by the adherents of these philosophies as "one of our own".

As Sedgwick argues, however, Laing's work in this early period can be distinguished from his later writings in three crucial respects. Firstly, there is no hint of mysticism in it. The book's key concept, *ontological insecurity*, for example simply means:

> [a] profound personal uncertainty about the boundaries between the self and the world, which can be contrasted with the differentiation of ego-boundaries which takes place in normal child development. "Being-in-the-world" means social interaction between persons and Kierkegaard's "Sickness unto Death" is not the loneliness of the soul before God but the despair of the psychotic. Laing is, in short, naturalising the mystical elements of continental existentialist thought.[145]

Secondly, in contrast to his later writings, there is no suggestion in *The Divided Self* that schizophrenia or other forms of severe mental distress, however conceptualised, are anything other than sheer affliction, let alone a heightened form of consciousness.

Thirdly, "schizophrenia" at this stage is still a pattern of responses manifested by the individual person. As Sedgwick comments:

> It has not vanished, as it does in the Laing of five years hence, into the criss-cross of distorted and distorting signals that typifies Laing's description of the patient's family in which no individual is "ill" or "schizophrenic" at all.[146]

### From *Self and Others* to *The Politics of Experience*

If *The Divided Self* (1960) was Laing's most "psychiatric" text, the publications which appeared over the next few years, including *Self and Others* (1961) and *Sanity, Madness and the Family* (1964), marked a shift away from a focus on the individual with a condition labelled "schizophrenia" to a focus on the relationships and transactions between that individual and others, specifically other family members.

In his foreword to the 1965 Pelican edition of *The Divided Self*, Laing could write:

> Even in focusing upon and attempting to delineate a certain type of schiz-oid existence, I was already falling into the trap I was seeking to avoid. [147]

That "trap" meant even conceding the very existence of a "condi-tion" called schizophrenia. By way of contrast, by the time of the publication of the second edition of *Sanity, Madness and the Family* (with Aaron Esterson, 1969), he felt able to assert that:

> We do not accept "schizophrenia" as being a biochemical, neurophysi-ological, psychological fact and we regard it as palpable error, in the present state of the evidence, to take it to be a fact. Nor do we assume its existence. Nor do we adopt it as a hypothesis. We propose no model of it. [148]

As we will see in the next chapter, challenging the theoretical and empirical validity of psychiatric categories such as schizophrenia is a central concern of the work of contemporary critical psychologists and psychiatrists such as Mary Boyle and Joanna Moncrieff. What was original and controversial about Laing's view, however, was the alterna-tive view of schizophrenia he put forward, summarised in *The Politics of Experience* (1967) as follows:

> There is no such "condition" as schizophrenia, but the label is a social fact and the social fact a *political event*. This political event, occurring in the civic order of society, imposes definitions and consequences on the labelled person. It is a social prescription that rationalises a set of social actions whereby the labelled person is annexed by others, who are legally sanctioned, medically empowered, and morally obliged, to become responsible for the person labelled. The person labelled is inau-gurated not only into a role, but into a career of patient, by the concerted action of a coalition (a "conspiracy") of family, GP, mental health officer, psychiatrists, nurses, psychiatric social workers and often fellow patients. [149]

Here, the influence both of Goffman's influential text *Asylums* and of the "labelling" theorists of the 1960s is evident. Quite why families and mental health systems should behave in this way, however, (what it is that they are reacting against?) is not made clear by Laing. Rather, he suggests, this and other questions "are only just beginning to be asked, much less answered".[150] What he does say, however, is that while until now, the answer has tended to be sought within the family, it is necessary to move beyond that layer of explanation and consider also

> [t]he meaning of all this within the larger context of the civic order of society—that is, of the *political order*, of the ways persons exercise control and power over one another.[151]

While this might suggest that Laing is moving towards a concrete political analysis of schizophrenia, in fact within the same paper his argument moves in precisely the opposite direction: towards "inner space". Here and elsewhere, from the mid-1960s onwards he begins, uniquely among psychiatrists, to put forward the idea of schizophrenia as a kind of "healing journey", an "inner voyage":

> Instead of the mental hospital, a sort of re-servicing factory for human breakdowns, we need a place where people who have travelled further, and consequently may be more lost than psychiatrists and other sane people, can find their way further into inner space and time, and back again. Instead of the degradation ceremonial of psychiatric examination, diagnosis and prognostication, we need, for those who are ready for it (in psychiatric terminology, often those who are about to go into a schizophrenic breakdown) an initiation ceremonial, through which the person will be guided with full social encouragement and sanction into inner space and time, by people who have been there and back again.[152]

If one should conclude from this that Laing was moving in the direction of mysticism, then that would be a correct conclusion. In this of course he was hardly alone; 1967—the year in which *the Politics of Experience* was published—was also for example the year in which the Beatles went off to India to study meditation with the Maharishi Mahesh Yogi. In addition, Laing was known to have shared LSD with the American gurus of the drug, Timothy Leary and Richard Alpert. And so his decision in 1971 to take himself off for a lengthy period to a monastery in what was then Ceylon to study Buddhist meditation should have come as no great surprise, given what he had written a few years earlier in the penultimate chapter of *The Politics of Experience*:

True sanity entails in one way or another the dissolution of the normal ego, that false self competently adjusted to our alienated social reality: the emergence of the "inner" archetypal mediators of divine power, and through this death a rebirth, and the eventual re-establishment of a new kind of ego-functioning, the ego now being the servant of the divine, no longer its betrayer.

## Assessing Laing

Some four decades on, it is difficult to convey the impact which Laing's ideas had on a layer of young people in the 1960s and early 1970s. One reason for the appeal of these ideas is suggested by the socialist-feminist psychoanalyst Juliet Mitchell in her discussion of Laing in *Psychoanalysis and Feminism*:

> In the early sixties, era of the problem of the teenage revolt, Laing, intentionally or not, took up the battle on behalf of the rebels. His works speak to the heart of the adolescent predicament. *They are about the crisis of leaving home.* This was not just a radical gesture of support on Laing's part—*the whole project and achievement of his "science of person" is dedicated to this end.*[153]

This is an over-statement. While it is undoubtedly true that Laing's writings did strike a chord with many young people who experienced their own family unit as oppressive, it is simplistic (and perhaps a bit patronising) in what is otherwise an insightful discussion of his ideas from a psychoanalytic perspective to reduce Laing's appeal to this aspect of his thought.

For a start, interest in, and enthusiasm for, the ideas of Laing went far beyond the ranks of young people—there was a veritable industry of books and articles, both academic and popular, about Laing during this period.

Secondly, young people in the 1960s did indeed have much to be angry about—the USA's ongoing brutal war in Vietnam, the denial of rights to black people in the Deep South, a nuclear arms race which threatened global annihilation, the crisis of homelessness in the UK exposed by TV dramas such as *Cathy Come Home* and much more. At least as much as his critique of the nuclear family, a strong element of Laing's appeal was his ability to expose the hypocrisy and contradictions of an official view of "sanity" which sanctioned and justified these horrors as "normal" while stigmatising as "mad" those whose mental health broke down under the stresses and strains of living in such a world. As the popular slogan of the period put it, "Do not adjust your mind— there is a fault in reality".

Above all, however, Laing's contribution was to show that if we look at serious mental illness (however defined) through the eyes of the person who is experiencing it, it can have a meaning which will not be at all apparent from a biomedical perspective. That emphasis on "the politics of experience" was to be central to the subsequent development of the mental health service user movement and more recent Mad Studies approaches. In this connection, Juliet Mitchell quotes Freud:

> [I]t seems plausible at first to expect that biochemistry will one day disclose a substance to us whose presence produces a male sexual excitation and another substance which produces a female one. But this hope seems no less naïve than the other one—happily obsolete today—that it may be possible under the microscope to isolate the different exciting factors of hysteria, obsessional neurosis, melancholia and so on.

She comments:

> Thanks to Laing, we can now add "schizophrenia" to his list, only lamenting that it takes so long to repeat a discovery and that we are still having to fight the naïve biochemists of male and female biological determinism.[154]

In reality, as we saw in Chapter 2, in the second decade of the 21st century the "naïve biochemists" are more firmly in the saddle than ever. While the demolition and demonisation of the ideas of Laing and of anti-psychiatry that took place in the 1970s was primarily the work of a resurgent biomedical psychiatry establishment (aided, it has to be said, by Laing's growing reliance on alcohol and his increasingly outlandish therapeutic practices, including the organisation of mass "re-birthing" events in the mid-1980s), criticism of Laing did not only come from biomedical psychiatry or the political right. It also came from the political left, above all from the pen of Peter Sedgwick. As noted above, Sedgwick's 1982 text *Psychopolitics* has recently been republished and been the subject of discussion and debate. Here, we shall revisit some of his key arguments.

## Psychopolitics

*Psychopolitics* is a book of three parts. The first part involves a critical exploration of the idea that mental illness is qualitatively different from physical illness. This is followed by a discussion of the ideas of four leading contemporary critics of psychiatry: the American psychiatrist Thomas Szasz, sociologist Erving Goffman, philosopher and historian Michel Foucault and R D Laing. The final part of the book addresses the question of what a more humane mental health system would look like and what might be involved in achieving it. Here our discussion will focus mainly on the first part of the book and on Sedgwick's critique of Laing.

Sedgwick begins by addressing the debate between supporters of psychiatry and their anti-psychiatry opponents concerning the nature of mental illness. For the former group, both physical and mental illnesses were to be viewed through a positivist lens, as biological "facts". In essence, schizophrenia and bipolar illness belonged to the same category as arthritis or multiple sclerosis. By contrast, the anti-psychiatrists saw physical illness as qualitatively different from so-called mental illness—the first was real, the second (in the title of Szasz's best-known book) a "myth", a social construction for which there were no biological markers.

Sedgwick critiqued both positions. The two groups, he argued, had failed to ask the logically prior question: what is illness? And in answer to that question, he suggested, *all* illnesses are social constructions:

"all sickness is essentially deviancy...there are no illnesses or diseases in nature."[155]

The point was most obvious, he argued, in relation to "mental illness":

To say that somebody is mentally ill, or to announce oneself as mentally ill, is to attach complex meanings to acts and behaviours that in other societies, or in different contingencies within our own society, would be interpreted in the light of quite different concepts.[156]

However, physical illness, he argued, was no less socially constructed. He used the example of tooth decay:

[A]mong millions of British working-class families, it is taken for granted that children will lose their teeth and require artificial dentures. The process of tooth loss is not seen as a disease but as something like an act of fate. Among dentists, on the other hand, and in those more educated sections of the community who are socialised into dental ideology, the loss of teeth arises through a definite disease process known as caries, whose aetiology is established.[157]

He summarised his position as follows:

*All* illness, whether conceived in localised bodily terms or within a larger view of human functioning, expresses both a social value judgment (contrasting a person's condition with understood and accepted norms) and an attempt at explanation (with a view to controlling this disvalued condition). The physicalistic psychiatrists are wrong in their belief that they can find objective disease entities representing the psychopathological analogues to diabetes, tuberculosis and post-syphylitic paresis. Quite correctly, the anti-psychiatrists have pointed out that psychopathological categories refer to value judgements and that mental illness is deviancy. On the other hand, the anti-psychiatric critics themselves are wrong when they imagine physical medicine to be essentially different in its logic from psychiatry. A diagnosis of diabetes, or paresis, includes the recognition of norms or values. Anti-psychiatry can only operate by positing a mechanical and inaccurate model of physical illness and its medical diagnosis. It follows therefore from the above train of argument that mental illnesses can be conceptualised within the disease framework just as easily as physical maladies such as lumbago or TB.[158]

As he recognised, it was an argument that could easily be subject to misunderstanding and so he went on to qualify it in two ways. Firstly, it was not an argument in support of the existing official categories of mental illness; thus, he suggested, it was likely that "schizophrenia"

[i]s a rudimentary dustbin category for a variety of psychic ills which may have little logically or biologically in common with each other.

Such diagnostic categories were invented or discarded in line with social, medical and historical changes:

I can see for example by the year 2081 nobody will be classed as having diabetes or asthma, though they will undergo feelings of discomfort similar to those experienced by present-day diabetics or asthmatics.[159]

Secondly, "and much more importantly" he stressed, he was not arguing for "the technologising of", for more treatments for specific conditions:

[T]he specialised medical model of illness is not the only one... The greatest advances in the control of disease have often come about through non-medical measures, and in particular through social and political change. The insertion of windows into working-class houses (with the consequent beneficial influx of sunlight), or the provision of a pure water supply and efficient sewage disposal, did more to clear up the plagues of modern epidemic infection than did the identification of particular microbes or the synthesis of medical discoveries, like the various antibiotics and antitoxins.[160]

For Sedgwick, however, the debate also had important political implications. In fact his primary concern was with what he saw as the social and political consequences of discarding the concept of mental illness:

I am arguing that, without the concept of illness—including that of mental illness since to exclude it would constitute the crudest dualism—we shall be unable to make demands on the health service facilities of the society we live in... Mental illness, like mental health, is a fundamentally *critical* concept: or can be made into one provided that those who use it are prepared to place demands and pressures on the existing organisation of society. In trying to remove and reduce the concept of mental illness, the revisionist theorists have made it that much harder for a powerful campaign of reform in the mental health services to get off the ground.[161]

Sedgwick then turned his attention to the ideas of the four thinkers noted above, with Szasz, Goffman and Foucault getting a chapter each and Laing two chapters. Here we shall confine ourselves to a discussion of two of the main points of Sedgwick's critique of Laing: the movement away from politics and towards mysticism, and the role of the family in "causing" schizophrenia.

Sedgwick suggests a continuity in Laing's thought from *The Divided Self* through to his embrace of mysticism in the late 1960s:

We may see the growth of his ideas as a sequence of challenges to the whole catalogue of "schizoid" symptoms which is customarily presented in psychiatric textbooks. Each manifestation of behaviour that in ortho-dox medicine is offered as a "sign" of clinical pathology is taken by Laing to be a comprehensible act which, when aligned against its social context, appears as eminently reasonable and sane.[162]

As we have seen, in *The Divided Self* that meant viewing the speech and the behaviour of the patient as evidence of a fragmented or split self. In his subsequent work, however, the focus of explanation shifts from the individual to the patient's social setting and his or her interactions with others—above all the family. Laing's journey does not stop there, however. His basic stance of what Sedgwick calls "solidarity with the schizophrenic" (and what was seen by others as the "romanticisa-tion" of psychosis) led him, Sedgwick argued, directly towards mysticism. For even after all the symptoms of schizophrenia have been validated and found meaningful:

> What are we to make of that peculiar syndrome of the dissolution of personality itself, the "loss of ego-boundaries" characteristic of so many severely deteriorated schizophrenics who literally do not know where they themselves leave off, and a reality exterior to them begins?[163]

Traditionally within both medical and psychoanalytic thought such loss of ego-boundaries has been seen as catastrophic. In line with his basic stance of validating the schizophrenic experience, however, Laing condemned the overemphasis in modern society on what he called "egoic experience" and appeared to accept the traditional Buddhist view of such egoic experience as "an illusion".

As Sedgwick commented:

> The alternative to downgrading the "egoic" (which appears to be a syno-nym for humanity's perception of and activity in the world of nature and society) would have been to admit that the loss of the boundary between "inner" and "outer", "ego" and "world" was a terrible misfortune; and this Laing could not do if he was to pursue his project of out-and-out solidarity with psychotic experience.[164]

Sedgwick's philosophical critique of Laing's embrace of mysticism was accompanied by a scathing political condemnation of Laing's deci-sion in the early 1970s to relocate to a monastery in a government-held area of Ceylon (what is now Sri Lanka), a country at that time in the grip of a brutal civil war and therefore an act which Sedgwick saw as a major political betrayal.

A second aspect of Laing's thought critiqued by Sedgwick was his view that the behaviours associated with the label schizophrenia were understandable ("intelligible") as a response to the skewed dynamics and communication patterns of particular families. In a revised version of a paper first presented in 1964 and included in *The Politics of Experience*, Laing claimed:

> In over 100 cases where we have studied the actual circumstances around the social event when one person comes to be regarded as schizophrenic, it seems to us that *without exception* the experience and behaviour that gets labelled schizophrenic is a *special strategy that a person invents in order to live in an unliveable situation.*[165]

Sedgwick rejected this argument on both scientific-empirical and ethico-political grounds: scientific-empirical in that Laing had failed to demonstrate, he argued, anything particularly unusual about the inter-actions of the families in the case studies (as well as failing to provide a promised comparative study of "normal" families), and ethico-political in that Laing wholly unjustifiably appeared to be blaming parents for driving their children crazy.

## A "Sedgwickian" mental health politics?

Sedgwick's views on mental health as presented in *Psychopolitics*, have gained a new audience in recent years to the extent that some critical academics and practitioners now identify themselves as "Sedgwickian" in their approach to mental health politics. The guest editors of a recent special issue of the journal *Critical and Radical Social Work*, for example, devoted to a discussion of Sedgwick's ideas explain his attraction for them as follows:

> Sedgwick was able to hold in tension the important insights of prevailing critical mental health discourse (this was often framed in "anti-psychiatry" rhetoric) whilst also problematising elements of this discourse, what he called "half-truths"... Sedgwick remains a challenging and sobering figure to would-be radicals because he was cautious of crude radical-sounding counter ideologies that might be imposed on those already suffering mental distress. We could argue that he

embodied the spirit of historical materialism—analyzing the actual dynamics of an unfolding social situation in the present—what he called the prevailing conditions of political possibility for social change.

Contributors to the special issue, including several leading contemporary commentators on mental health issues, variously claim Sedgwick as a precursor of "Mad Studies"[166] or as a "proto-critical realist".[167]

The richness of Sedgwick's book and the sharpness of his insights particularly into the limitations of anti-psychiatry should be evident from the discussion above. Its arguments are particularly relevant at a time when mental health services are under attack as a consequence of austerity policies. As Cresswell and Spandler have noted, however, there is a danger of treating Sedgwick's ideas with undue reverence, quite in opposition to the spirit of his own approach. In this final section I will address what I believe to be some of the weaknesses in Sedgwick's critique of Laing and anti-psychiatry.

Firstly, there is his conflation of physical and mental illness. While Sedgwick was right to seek to avoid a mind/body dualism and to point to the socially constructed nature of both physical and mental illness, to *equate* the two risks ignoring one of the most important features of mental distress (and one which Laing explored brilliantly in *The Divided Self*)—namely, the subjective experience of distress and how one responds to it. Most people, for example, would react to hearing persecutory voices inside their head with fear and paranoia, responses that will often be mistaken for "madness". Similarly, Brown and Harris's 1978 study of depression in women concluded that what mattered in the genesis of this condition was not simply the experience of changes in one's life (such as divorce or bereavement) but rather how one made sense of such changes—their meaning:

> Change in itself is of no importance—everything turns on the meaningfulness of events... For change to be important it had to be associated with long-term threat which in turn usually involved loss and disappointment.[168]

As one perceptive commentator on anti-psychiatry, Zbigniew Kotowicz, has argued:

> In the course of his discussion Sedgwick raises several important issues, but his analysis is incomplete, so incomplete in fact that it may render

some of his conclusions spurious. Nowhere in his deliberations is the difference between *experiencing* a mental and physical illness examined. It may well be, and most probably is, that the difference between contracting pneumonia, for example, and having a nervous breakdown is such that it calls for widely divergent responses.[169]

While there are definite limits to a "politics of experience", validating people's personal experience of madness and mental distress (as well as their experience of the psychiatric system) provided an essential starting point not only for Laing but also for the psychiatric survivors' movement of recent decades.

Secondly, whatever the weaknesses of Laing's theories, he did at least put forward an explanation for the development of psychosis in individuals. By contrast, Sedgwick offers no such argument. As Kotowicz notes:

[O]ften his arguments reduce the problem to the question of dealing with the mentally disabled, without ever analyzing how people get to the stage of chronic disablement.[170]

In fact, his hostility to the arguments of the anti-psychiatrists on the one hand and his desire to express solidarity with families of the mentally unwell on the other, evidenced by his active involvement in and support for the National Schizophrenia Association, a family organisation strongly committed to a biological model of schizophrenia, occasionally involved him in a fairly uncritical defence of the then dominant psychiatric practices. So, for example, in a review for *Socialist Worker* of David Mercer's 1972 movie *Family Life*, a drama-documentary based on Laingian theories, he wrote:

*Family Life* panders to the common prejudices which create the stigma of mental illness. It tries to persuade us that there really is something horrific and shameful about seeking medical help during a time of emotional distress; that to submit to a controlled state of unconsciousness which may afford temporary (but essential) relief from a personal nightmare—which is what electroshock therapy does when properly administered—is some kind of surrender to the ruling class; that to take a tranquilising pill or injection—again perhaps for relief rather than for any profound cure—is to accept conformity with the goals of our hateful social system.[171]

Thirdly, there is the *tone* of Sedgwick's critique. While he is correct to highlight the political and theoretical shortcomings of Szasz, Goffman, Foucault and Laing and to demonstrate the limits of their radicalism, he comes close to throwing out the baby with the bathwater; the "baby" in this case being their often valid and important insights into the oppressive nature of the dominant biomedical psychiatry. Kotowicz again:

> Sedgwick's denunciation of anti-psychiatry is merciless. He leaves no stone unturned in seeking out the failings of the movement. Many of his observations are important, particularly his analysis of the libertarian free-market psychiatry as envisaged by Szasz; there is always a need to remind the public that some of the rhetoric of freedom conceals a wish to return to a Darwinian society. But while almost all criticisms are pertinent, there is also something disquieting about the tone—disdain, scorn, mockery, curt dismissal. After all, these thinkers have helped enormously in alerting the public to the issues of psychiatry, even if ideologically some of them are not acceptable.[172]

This is particularly true of his critique of Laing. Whatever the methodological shortcomings of books such as *Sanity, Madness and the Family*, Laing deserves credit for his attempts both to understand, and to show solidarity with, one of the most oppressed and stigmatised groups in society. In addition, his argument that the pressures and dynamics of family life can be highly damaging to the mental health of their members is surely not contentious. Philip Larkin's assertion that "They fuck you up, your mum and dad. They may not mean to, but they do" is one that many people will readily recognise from their own experience, while as early as 1972 a group of mainstream psychiatrists and academics were developing what became known as "Expressed Emotion theory", identifying the role of families in the relapse (if not causation) of schizophrenia.[173] Laing himself was generally careful to avoid saying that families *cause* schizophrenia, or at least not consciously:

> Nor is it a matter of laying the blame at anyone's door. The untenable position, the "can't win" double-bind, the situation of checkmate, is by definition *not obvious* to the protagonists. Very seldom is it a question of contrived, deliberate, cynical lies or a ruthless intention to drive someone crazy, although this occurs more commonly than is usually supposed.[174]

Finally, underpinning Sedgwick's critique was a political concern, noted above, that to dispense with the concept of "mental illness" would leave the left with no firm basis on which to defend existing mental health services or to fight for improved services. The same argument can be heard today when bodies such as the Royal College of Psychiatrists argue that mental health services should receive the same priority—and the same funding—as physical health services.

There is both a philosophical and a political response to this argument. Firstly, in terms of the "reality" or otherwise of madness or mental distress, the critical realist position put forward by David Pilgrim offers an alternative both to the illness model and to crude deviancy approaches which see conditions such as schizophrenia as simply a form of labelling and social control. Supporters of the biomedical model, including many psychiatrists, Pilgrim argues, make the error (he calls it the "epistemic fallacy")

> of confusing the (professionally preferred) map with the territory. So, for example, there is little scientific coherence in the concept of "schizophrenia" but some people do hear voices not heard by others present or they have fixed and rigid assumptions that make little sense to their peers. "Schizophrenia" does not exist as a thing—it is a (very poor) *concept* that, for political reasons, the medical profession retains and then (wrongly) attributes with conceptual and empirical validity. However, its constituent experiential features ("single symptoms" or "complaints") are recurring aspects of being alive for some people. This is why some people who reject psychiatric knowledge prefer a "single symptom" or "complaints" approach to mental health problems (eg Bentall, 2009).[175]

Thus the *experience* of hearing voices or feeling depressed, for example, are very real, but portraying this as illness can be unhelpful and misleading.

Politically, there is an important element of truth in Sedgwick's argument. When extremely unwell individuals are forced to travel hundreds of miles to secure a bed in a psychiatric hospital (as they frequently are at present in England), then fighting to defend—and improve—existing provision should be a political priority. Nor should we allow progressive-sounding models of mental health which stress notions of "independence" and "recovery" to be used as a smokescreen for cuts to services. That said, however, as numerous campaigns over the past decade to defend mental health services from cuts and closures have shown, service users, in alliance with trade unionists and campaigning organisations like the Social Work Action Network (SWAN), are much more likely to fight to defend services which they feel provide emotional and social support, as opposed to services which are experienced as oppressive and over-medicalised. In the words of the SWAN Charter for Mental Health:

> We need more alliances...to stop cuts and privatisation and ensure people are not denied access to properly resourced community and inpatient services. However it is not enough to save services as they are, we want them to be *better*. This means services shaped by users with democracy and participation at the centre. Interventions based on social approaches and that challenge discrimination. Support driven by social justice rather than the profit motive. Joint campaigns by service users, carers, practitioners, trade unionists and activists have the potential not only to defend but also to transform services.[176]

## Concluding comments

In a period when there are few reasons to be cheerful regarding issues of mental health, the above chapter points to two resources of hope. Firstly, the current crisis in mental health (or more accurately, *crises*, since the issue is not simply one of the extent of mental distress but also the nature and availability of mental health services) is leading service users, practitioners and commentators to revisit the debates and discussions of earlier decades and to explore the ideas of major radical thinkers such as R D Laing and Peter Sedgwick, as well as others not considered here for reasons of space, such as Franco Basaglia[177] and Franz Fanon.[178] It is crucial that we approach such debates in an open and non-sectarian spirit. All of these thinkers have their strengths and weaknesses. Only through critical and non-reverential debate and discussion can we identify those of their insights which are relevant today and those which can be discarded.

Secondly, Laing's major works were written in the 1960s when many of those diagnosed as mentally ill were still confined, voluntarily or involuntarily, in large asylums. Sedgwick's main political intervention in the area of mental health was with relatives' organisations, notably the National Schizophrenia Fellowship. Neither thinker seriously envisaged the possibility that the collective agency of people with mental health problems, or survivors of the psychiatric system, could be a force for change (and in this respect, the experience of Franco Basaglia and his colleagues in Italy in the 1970s and 1980s recently explored by John Foot has much to offer).[179] The emergence, then, of a mental health service user movement in recent decades, linked to the wider disability movement, marks a huge step forward. It means that the voices of those who are experiencing, or have experienced, mental distress should now always be at the heart of debates and discussions about the future of mental health provision and strategy. The possibilities inherent in that movement, as well as some of the debates within it, will be considered in the next chapter.

# 5

# "Bad things happen to you and drive you crazy": new challenges to psychiatric hegemony

## Introduction

By the end of the 1970s, the ideas of R D Laing and of anti-psychiatry more generally were in decline. That decline was due to a combination of the inconsistencies discussed in the previous chapter, a resurgent biomedical model and, above all, the wider retreat of radical movements following the election of Margaret Thatcher as prime minister in the UK and Ronald Reagan as president in the USA. The period since the beginning of the present century, however, has seen the emergence of new radical currents in mental health.

One of these involves a coalition of critical psychiatrists and psychologists, social workers, activists and service users who have contributed to what they describe as a "paradigm shift" in the understanding of mental health and mental distress. In place of a model which explains mental distress in terms of biochemical or genetic processes, the new paradigm, or worldview, locates "madness" and mental distress more generally primarily in people's life experiences:

A new and profoundly important paradigm for understanding overwhelming emotional pain has emerged over the last few years, with the potential to change the way we conceptualise human suffering across the whole spectrum of mental health difficulties. It is a strongly evidence-based synthesis of findings from trauma studies, attachment theory and neuroscience, which offers new hope for recovery. It also presents a powerful challenge to biomedical model psychiatry in that it is based on scientific evidence that substantiates and attests to what many individual with first-hand experience of mental health problems have always known—that the bad things that happen to you can drive you mad.[180]

Underpinning this new paradigm is a body of research-based evidence developed over the past decade primarily by critical psychologists and psychiatrists but also by social scientists such as Richard Wilkinson and Kate Pickett. These writers both highlight the limitations of the biomedical model and also advocate an alternative social model of mental distress rooted in people's life experience. The social work academic Jerry Tew sums up its key elements as follows:

> Whatever may be its biomedical correlates in terms of brain functioning and whatever part may be played by genetically derived sensitivities, we start with the foundational position that mental distress may be understood as a meaningful response to life circumstances. Specific distress experiences ("symptoms") may be understood as coping mechanisms—but ones that seem to have taken on a momentum of their own and which may come at a price in terms of levels of subjective distress, confusion and impaired functioning. They may also be seen as "intermediary languages" that are seeking to express some of the pent-up reality of social experiences that have become intolerable.[181]

So for example, cutting and other forms of self-harm would be understood within this framework as coping mechanisms, ways of dealing with emotional pain and releasing intolerable feelings which may be open to negotiation, rather than simply irrational or self-destructive acts.

The first part of this chapter will discuss some of the key elements of this proposed new paradigm and assess how well it makes sense of the realities of mental distress.

A second challenge, to be discussed later in this chapter, derives less from the writings and research of professionals and academics and more from the lived experience of people with mental health problems. As we saw in Chapter 2, historically a defining feature of the history of mental health services has been their tendency to discount or invalidate the thoughts and feelings of those experiencing madness and mental distress. Since the 1980s, however, there has been a growing challenge to that invalidation by people who use services (and some professional allies). In the wake of the emergence in the 1970s of a disability movement which located the sources of oppression and disadvantage in the structures of capitalist society rather than in individual impairment, a mental health users' movement has developed which similarly challenges the biomedical model and the medicalised responses which it promotes.

One example of that challenge has been the growth in the UK and internationally of Hearing Voices Networks, based on the finding by Dutch psychiatrist Marius Romme, psychologist Sandra Escher and service user Patsy Hage that "hearing voices" inside one's head is a much wider phenomenon than was previously recognised. Such voices, Romme and his colleagues have argued, will often be a response to traumatic life experiences and can be responded to in ways that do not rely on psychotropic medication. The nature and significance of the mental health users' movement, as well as some of the political debates to which it has given rise, will be considered in the second part of the chapter. Before then, however, it is necessary to outline and critically assess the new paradigm referred to above.

## Challenging the dominant paradigm

The new paradigm is underpinned by four key concepts: trauma, dissociation, attachment and neuroscience. The first three will be considered here and the fourth later in the discussion.

### Trauma

In her study of liberation psychology in Latin America, Nancy Hollander defines trauma as

> the disruption or breakdown of the psychic apparatus when it is affected by stimuli, external or internal, that are too powerful to be dealt with or assimilated in customary ways.[182]

Hollander's discussion is set in the context of the brutal repression, violence and torture experienced by tens of thousands of people across Latin America during the years of military rule in the 1970s and 1980s. But trauma can also take much more everyday forms. Evidence suggests that there is a strong causal link, for example, between childhood adversity and trauma on the one hand and severe mental distress or psychosis in later life on the other. Summarising the research in this area, Richard Bentall has argued:

> Recent studies have pointed to a wide range of social and environmental factors that increase the risk of mental ill-health. These

include poverty in childhood, social inequality and early exposure to urban environments; migration and belonging to an ethnic minority (all trending in the wrong direction); early separation from parents; childhood sexual, physical and emotional abuse; and bullying in schools.

In an analysis of all the research on childhood trauma and psychosis, my colleagues and I found that exposure to any of these childhood adversities increased the risk of psychosis approximately three-fold, and those who had multiple traumatic experiences were at much higher risk. In fact, the evidence of a link between childhood misfortune and future psychiatric disorder is about as strong statistically as the link between smoking and lung cancer.[183]

Two other findings are worth emphasising. Firstly, it appears that *specific* symptoms of conditions such as schizophrenia are often linked to childhood trauma and adversity:

Symptoms considered indicative of psychosis and schizophrenia, such as hallucinations, are at least as strongly related to childhood abuse and neglect as many other mental health problems.[184]

Secondly, and reversing the causal relationship asserted by supporters of biomedical approaches, Bentall argues that changes in the brains of people diagnosed as schizophrenic are often a response to the effects of such trauma and adversity, not the other way round:

There is also now strong evidence that these kinds of experiences affect brain structure, explaining many of the abnormal neuro-imaging findings that have been reported for psychiatric patients.

Psychiatrist John Read makes a similar point in a paper on childhood adversity and psychosis:

The evidence is that all the structural and functional differences between the brains of "schizophrenics" and "normal" adults (which are cited to support the "brain-disease" hypothesis) are the same differences found between young children who have been traumatised and those who have not. These include: over-activity of the hypothalamic-adrenal-pituitary axis; dopamine, serotonin and norepinephrine abnormalities; and structural differences such as hippo-campal damage, cerebral atrophy, ventricular enlargements and reversed cerebral asymmetry.[185]

What the research evidence in this area shows, Read concludes, is that:

> Most or all mental health problems have their roots in childhood and that "schizophrenia" and psychosis, contrary to decades of claims that they are bio-genetically based, are no exception.

The importance of early experience in respect of the diagnosis of "personality disorder" was also highlighted in a 2005 study into the links between homelessness and mental health problems conducted by University of Stirling researchers which quoted one experienced clinician as follows:

> In fact I would go as far as to say that I can't think of any patients I've seen in the last two and a half years of the homeless population who described what you might call a normal upbringing. And I'm not exaggerating, I really can't think of anyone.[186]

This does not mean that all mental distress is reducible to, or determined by, adverse events in childhood. What it does suggest though is that such events may create a *vulnerability* to mental health problems which may then be triggered by later adverse life experiences or stresses. This is not dissimilar to the "biopsychosocial" or "stress-vulnerability" model developed in the 1970s in an attempt to overcome the weaknesses of the medical model. One problem with that model, however, was that the dominance of biological thinking meant that in practice it was assumed that the vulnerability had to be *genetic* (leading some critics to dub it the "biobiobio" model of psychosis).[187] As Read and Sanders argue:

> This reduced social factors like child abuse, unemployment, loss, poor living conditions, etc to mere triggers of an underlying genetic or constitutional time-bomb—only people who had the supposed genetic or constitutional predispositions would become depressed, alcoholic, mad, etc, it implied that social factors by themselves cannot cause mental health problems.

In reality, as they go on to argue:

Although we are, of course, born with genetic variations (including, quite probably, variations in our general sensitivity to stress) you don't need a genetic predisposition for bad things happening to overwhelm you, make you depressed or drive you crazy.[188]

Finally, as Bentall points out, even those who have enjoyed the most idyllic childhoods, can still experience mental health problems:

And of course there are myriad adult adversities that also contribute to mental ill-health, including debt, unhappy marriages, excessively demanding work environments and the threat of unemployment. Arguably the biggest cause of human misery is miserable relationships with other people, conducted in miserable circumstances.[189]

## Dissociation

A second component of the proposed new paradigm is *dissociation*. According to one leading writer on Post-Traumatic Stress Syndrome (PTSD):

Dissociation is the essence of trauma. The overwhelming experience is split off and fragmented, so that the emotions, sounds, images, thoughts and physical sensation related to the trauma take on a life of their own. The sensory fragments of memory intrude into the present where they are literally relived.[190]

It is not difficult to see why the concept of dissociation should play an important role in this alternative paradigm. Both the feelings (and in some cases, the behaviours) following trauma are similar to those which would be associated with psychotic conditions such as schizo-phrenia. As Van der Kolk comments:

These reactions are irrational and largely outside people's control. Intense and barely controllable urges and emotions make people feel crazy—and make them feel they don't belong to the human race. Feeling numb during birthday parties for your kids or in response to the death of loved ones makes people feel like monsters. As a result, shame becomes the dominant emotion and hiding the truth the central preoccupation.[191]

At the same time, as Dillon and her colleagues argue, like psychosis, dissociation can also have a protective function, acting as "a protective device that permits individuals to detach mentally from experiences that are too overwhelming for the psyche to process".[192]

## Attachment theory

A third element in the new paradigm (though in itself far from new) is *attachment*. Originating in the post-war studies of the psychiatrist John Bowlby on separation, attachment and loss, attachment theory emphasises the central role played by early formative relationships with a caregiver on a baby's social, emotional and cognitive development and also on his or her later mental health. Dillon defines attachment as:

> A stable progression of cognitive, affective and behavioural styles that persist into adulthood, creating an interpersonal template that underpins one's ability to relate to others, regulate emotion, mentalise (infer the mental state of others) and manage autonomic arousal in order to cope with threatening feelings and situations.

While those who have experienced positive early relationships are more likely to develop secure attachment styles making them more likely to show resilience in the face of life's adversities, it is argued, those who have had more negative experiences may develop coping styles (classified as avoidant, ambivalent or disorganised) which not only make them less able to handle difficulties but also (allegedly) make them more prone to mental health problems, including psychosis.

## Assessing the new paradigm

A model of mental distress which recognises—and provides empirical evidence for—the causal role played by early life experience, poverty, inequality, racism, sexism and other forms of oppression in the genesis of mental health problems is a huge step forward from a model which locates such problems primarily in faulty genes or biochemical deficiencies. The fact also that the new paradigm does not discount genes, brains and biochemistry but rather emphasises the interaction between our brains and our environments, including the ways in which brain structure is shaped by life experiences, also allows for a much more dialectical understanding of mental distress:

> [T]he new paradigm sees body and mind as mutually interactive, reflecting and reinforcing each other... Since biological factors are not

privileged as primary and causal in a simplistic, reductive way, what we have outlined is not an illness model but a psychosocial trauma model, with very different implications for intervention.[193]

Some of these implications for intervention will be considered in the final chapter. That said, the new model is not without potential limitations.

Firstly, while the emphasis on trauma roots mental distress in actual life experiences, this does not automatically lead to a more political understanding of mental distress. As the history of the diagnosis PTSD shows, it may simply involve replacing a depoliticised, individualised, *biological* diagnosis with a depoliticised, individualised, *psychological* diagnosis. As Jonathan Neale shows in his study of the Vietnam War, the diagnosis was originally developed to make sense of the mental distress of a sizeable minority of US Vietnam Veterans, distress which included re-living their distressing experiences as memories or dreams, becoming emotionally numb and experiencing insomnia and irritability. Rather than linking such distress, however, to the imperialist motives which led these young men to be in Vietnam in the first place and the murderous behaviours that such involvement demanded of them, the diagnosis, particularly in the Freudian-influenced centre where it was developed, explained their distress as resulting from (unconscious) guilt at having done terrible things and enjoying doing them—blamed them, in other words, for their condition:

> The center treated men wounded by the war but it was a government center. It could not say "The officers and the government are to blame". It could not say "What has been done to you in Vietnam is of a piece with what has been done to you since". And it could not allow the patients to say those things. So the psychiatric theory blamed the men. They wanted to kill.[194]

Similarly, the radical Latin American psychologists and psychoanalysts Hollander interviewed for her study *Love in a Time of Hate* chose not to use the term PTSD because they saw it as individualising what was in reality a collective experience, resulting from living under military dictatorship:

> We do not think the concept of PTSD is an adequate one to describe the psychological impact of state terror. It makes a psychiatric problem out of

a social phenomenon…we don't even speak of trauma because it is usually understood to mean an intrapsychic experience. We use the concept "traumatic situation" in order to represent the social sources of the psychological suffering produced by state terror… The essence of social trauma is that it is not a private but is a public and shared experience.[195]

Clearly the collective mental health of a people under military dictatorship will be very different from that experienced by people living in the conditions of bourgeois democracy. But the more general point—the danger of individualising and depoliticising conditions which are the result of social phenomena and problems—still applies.

Secondly, the stress on the importance of attachment for mental health during the early months or years of life can lead to policy conclusions which are neither necessarily accurate or progressive, especially when linked to dubious (or simply wrong) interpretations of the findings of neuroscience. The emphasis on "early intervention" by the state in the lives of children, for example, has been a key policy plank of both New Labour and Conservative governments in the UK for over a decade. No one would argue against providing additional support and resources for parents to help them bring up their children. There were many positive aspects, for example, to the Sure Start programme launched by New Labour governments after 1997. But as Steven and Hilary Rose have argued, the motives behind such early intervention programmes—and the assumptions which underpin them—are sometimes neither benign nor scientifically founded.[196]

One important driver, for example, has been wealth creation and increasing the competitiveness of the British economy. The Roses cite an influential report published by the New Labour government in 2008 entitled *Mental Capital and Wellbeing: Making the Most of Ourselves in the 21st Century*:

> "Countries must learn how to capitalise on their citizens' cognitive resources if they are to prosper, both economically and socially. Early intervention will be the key". And neuroscience is crucial to the project of changing for the better the minds of the young.[197]

The way in which neuroscience, linked to attachment theory, is politically deployed in this project is evident in a 2010 government-commissioned report by Labour MP Graham Allen entitled *Early Intervention: Smart*

*Investment, Massive Savings* which was published in 2011 and built on an earlier report jointly written by Allen and right wing Tory MP and former Conservative Party leader Iain Duncan Smith.[198]

The cover of the 2011 report shows MRI photographs of two brains, the first showing the healthy brain of a "normal" child, the other purporting to show the much smaller, more shrivelled brain of an extremely neglected child. The photographs are used to support Allen's argument that:

> [B]abies are born with 25 percent of their brains developed, and there is then a rapid period of development so that by the age of 3 their brains are 80 percent developed. In that period, neglect, the wrong type of parenting and other adverse experiences can have a profound effect on how children are emotionally "wired".[199]

Damaged brains are then linked to attachment theory to pin the blame squarely where it supposedly belongs—not on poverty or lack of resources but instead on feckless parents:

> Parents who are neglectful or who are drunk, drugged or violent, will have impaired capacity to provide this social and emotional stability, and will create the likelihood that adverse experiences might have a negative impact on their children's development...the worst and deepest damage is done to children when their brains are being formed during their earliest months and years.[200]

It is a short step from here to arguing that, in the words of Barnardo's Chief Executive, Martin Narey:

> More babies should be removed from their mothers at birth before irreparable harm is inflicted. There is an argument to be made...that even intervening at this early stage is too late.[201]

As critics have argued, this is right wing social policy masquerading as science. Firstly, questions have been raised about the origins of the widely circulated and influential MRI images which adorn the front of Allen's report, images which as the Roses point out:

> Are far more dramatic, for example, than anything seen amongst the desperately impoverished children rescued from Romanian orphanages in the 1990s following the fall of the Ceaucescu regime.[202]

In fact, in response to their enquiries the author of the original research which included the photographs has since distanced himself from the Allen report, claiming that his findings were "distorted".

Secondly, in terms of the science underpinning the arguments of the early interventionists, it is worth quoting the views of Hilary and Steven Rose, two of the leading authorities in this area, at some length:

> The Early Intervention assumptions are: (1) The more synapses [structures that permit a nerve cell or neuron to pass a message to another nerve cell] the better; (2) Poor environments in these critical years permanently reduce synapse numbers and the brain doesn't wire up properly; (3) There are critical (or sensitive) periods in brain development, especially; (4), for proper attachment bonds to be formed between caregiver (mother) and infant; (5) "toxic stress" at this early period has lasting consequences for later development. Neither of the first two is supported by the neuroscientific evidence; the third, fourth and fifth oversimplify very complex relationships between the child's developing brain and environmental context.[203]

Similarly Michael Rutter, probably the leading global authority on attachment theory, has distanced himself from what he describes as the "evangelism" behind claims that "early years determine brain development". In a presidential address to the Society for Research on Child Development, he drew (as do the Roses) on the philosopher John Bruer's *The Myth of the First Three Years* (1999) to assert that "the claims of advocates of early intervention are misleading and fallacious...the assumption that later experiences necessarily have only minor effects is clearly wrong".[204]

In fact as Steven and Hilary Rose argue, the key factor shaping children's neurological—as well as social, emotional and cognitive development—is class. They cite a collaborative US study which took place in 2015 involving both neuroscientists and social scientists which examined the development of children's brains in relation to socioeconomic status:

> The team studied 1,099 "typically developing" youngsters between the ages of three and twenty, and found that the surface area of the brain was related to family income. Amongst poorer families, a small increase in income increased brain area significantly—especially in brain areas

associated with language and reading skills. If the family was rich then an increase in family income made little difference. The implication is that the simplest and most effective of early interventions to increase mental capital would be to lift children out of poverty. What has been happening in UK policy since the election of the Conservative Party, initially as a coalition Government in 2010, is precisely the reverse: more children are being pushed into poverty...while the government officially abandons the pledge to lift all out of poverty by 2020.[205]

## The mental health service user movement: "nothing about us without us"

The second major challenge to the dominant psychiatric worldview comes from a different group of people (although there is considerable overlap of ideas and personnel with the first group). The anti-psychiatry movement of the 1960s and 1970s was primarily a professional-led movement, shaped by radical psychiatrists and other mental health professionals. Its ideas, however, contributed to the emergence of a mental health users' movement, made up mainly of people who had themselves experienced mental health problems and who, for good or ill, had been on the receiving end of psychiatric services. (Supportive professionals or "allies" also contributed to the movement's development).

The material pre-condition for that movement was the dramatic shift that took place in mental health policy and provision in the 1950s and 1960s from institutional care to community care. Whatever the strengths or limitations of the old psychiatric hospitals, they could hardly be said to provide an environment conducive to organising around grievances. As the writer and historian Barbara Taylor, who spent periods as an in-patient in Friern Barnet psychiatric hospital in North London in the 1980s and subsequently attended a day hospital, writes of her experience:

> The idea of doing anything staff *didn't* like was unthinkable to me—and my fearfulness was by no means untypical or unreasonable. Even at the day hospital, and even in my case, mental patients were almost power-less. We could be drugged, transferred between institutions, detained in hospital—all without our consent or even our prior knowledge. The

popular present day slogan—"no decision about us without us"—was a distant dream for servicer users back in the 1980s.[206]

The first stirrings of revolt took place in the 1970s with the creation of a Mental Patients' Union by patients at the Paddington Day Hospital in 1973. Similar developments took place in Glasgow and elsewhere in the UK around the same time. In the period since then, a wide variety of groups and organisations have sprung up including the Campaign Against Psychiatric Oppression, Survivors Speak Out and the Hearing Voices Network, some short-lived, some more long-lasting, some national or even international. As I argued in an earlier assessment of this movement:

> While the nature of the mental health users' movement makes it diffi-cult to estimate the actual numbers of users or former users involved, one activist has estimated that the number of user groups has grown from around a dozen in the mid-1980s to around 350 nation-wide by the mid-1990s. (Campbell, 1996). Not all of these groups are campaign-ing groups. In her account of the movement, Lindow classifies them as *reactive* (advocacy projects, campaigning organisations), *alternative* (crisis centres, user-controlled projects) and *creative* (including Hearing Voices groups or Survivors' Poetry). What is likely to characterise all, or most of them, however, is the active involvement of users or former users of services in activities which to some degree challenge dominant, negative stereotypes of people with mental health problems.[207]

In the UK the quarterly magazine *Asylum* continues to provide a platform for the views of some of these groups and reports on their activities. And in response to the UK government's war on people on benefits since 2010 which has targeted people with mental health problems, new campaigning groups have emerged including Black Triangle (in Scotland), the Mental Health Resistance Network and Recovery in the Bin.

Organising a movement to challenge oppression in all its dimen-sions—material, political and ideological—is a huge task for any oppressed group of people, be it women, people with physical impair-ments, LGBT communities or black and minority ethnic groups. People with mental health problems face all these challenges and more.

So, for example, there is the stigma still associated with mental health issues. In terms of employment, 67 percent of respondents in a 2013 study by the organisation Time to Change said fear of stigma had stopped them from telling their employer or prospective employer about their mental health problems. In another study, conducted in 2009, 92 percent of the public thought someone's employment prospects would be damaged if they admitted to having a mental health problem.[208] This suggests that if governments were serious about helping people with mental health problems get back into the workplace, they should be focusing on challenging the discriminatory attitudes of employers rather than coercing individuals into work through benefit sanctions and work capability assessments. It also shows that for many people "coming out" in the workplace and community as having a mental health problem, let alone getting involved in building a movement, continues to be seen as just too risky.

A further challenge in organising service users (though one that should not be exaggerated) is the impact of mental distress itself. As one leading activist in the Scottish Mental Health Users' Network interviewed in 1997 as part of a study of the service user movement in Scotland put it:

> We face all the usual pressures that apply to any organisation but with an extra layer—our own mental health problems. The pressures mean that feelings can be more difficult to handle—that can create instability.[209]

A member of a mental health centre in Ayrshire highlighted other challenges involved in organising:

> I'm here because I've no confidence. You see other people, they say "G was a union man". But when you're in the hospital, you depend on the staff to help you, you look up to them. So when it comes to shouting the odds, you've no self-confidence. You can't go out into the street and walk up and down with a placard and shout "I'm daft—what are you going to do about it?" You've had no self-confidence in the first place—you hide away.[210]

It was such challenges that led even strong supporters of mental health service users like Peter Sedgwick to be pessimistic about the possibilities of their organising into a social movement. In fact, the willingness of hundreds, or even thousands, of people to "come out" about their own mental health problems over the past three decades and to fight for better services has made such a movement a reality, albeit one which, like all social movements, experiences ups and downs. Writing in the mid-1990s, Peter Campbell pointed to the material and organisational basis for the movement's growth:

> Since 1980 the mental health system in the United Kingdom (UK) has changed dramatically. While the main types of care and treatment provided by mental health services have changed little, the location of services and mechanism of delivery have undergone significant altera-tion. Simultaneously and partly as a direct result of these transformations, those diagnosed as mentally ill, the current and former mental health patients have become more visible and vocal within soci-ety and within the corridors of power. Government seeks their views. The service provider is obliged to consult with them.[211]

As an example, there was substantial service user involvement in the preparation of the Mental Health (Care and Treatment) (Scotland) Act 2003, widely seen as a progressive piece of mental health legislation (albeit one which introduced for the first time in Scotland compulsory treatment in the community, a measure opposed by most user groups and professional organisations).

So there has been progress, reflected in the creation of national organisations such as Shaping Our Lives; in public anti-stigma cam-paigns such as the See Me campaign in Scotland; in the emergence of new crisis services and social centres, usually located in the voluntary sector; and in government policies based on notions of recovery and independent living which, on paper at least, sound positive.

But as is usually the case with reforms under capitalism, the reality is often "one step forward, two steps back". Thus, the mental health policy papers of both Conservative and New Labour governments from the early 1990s onwards were stuffed full of progressive-sounding terms like "empowerment" and "user involvement". Yet while there have been good examples of service users shaping new and imaginative services in different areas of health and social care, for many the overall experience has been one of tokenism, of the appearance of participation rather than the reality, with power and control remaining in the hands of the state (or increasingly, of large private providers). As Branfield and Beresford noted in a review of service user involvement for the Joseph Rowntree Foundation in 2006:

There has been an increasing emphasis in recent years on user involvement in health and social care policy and practice. However, it has come in for growing questioning. Service providers and researchers have begun to ask what evidence there is that it improves services. Service users and their organisations have raised the issue of what they are actually able to achieve by their involvement and to question the usefulness of getting involved.[212]

That was written before the economic crash of 2008 and the imposition of the austerity policies which have resulted in the withdrawal of funding from many of the voluntary sector projects which were at the forefront of developing new forms of mental health service provision. To speak now of "user involvement" when, as we saw in Chapter 1, even the most basic forms of traditional psychiatric care are lacking, never mind more progressive services, seems like a bad joke. In 2013 in Glasgow, for example, service users fought the closure of the Charlie Reid Centre, a much-valued, long-standing mental health café and drop-in centre with over 300 members. One reason given for the closure was that the Centre was duplicating services already on offer from another local provider, Glasgow Association for Mental Health (GAMH). Having closed down the Charlie Reid Centre, however, the Labour-controlled Council then came back with a proposed 40 percent cut to the funding of GAMH! Only a vigorous campaign which united service users, GAMH workers, trade unions and organisations like the Social Work Action Network succeeded in reducing the cut to 30 percent, still a huge cut which has meant a reduction or withdrawal of service for many vulnerable people. Since then, the council's decision to implement cuts of £180 million over the following three years has led to further cuts to mental health and other services in the city.

Elsewhere in the UK, the threat of cuts to mental health services has also been met with resistance. In Norwich, for example, a well organised local campaign, which has now been running for several years, called a March for Mental Health in January 2016 involving hundreds of local people,[213] while in Cambridge in 2014, an occupation by a group of women service users was successful in preventing the closure of a much-valued day service.[214] These initiatives, like the Glasgow campaign, show the potential for building broad-based campaigns which go well beyond those immediately affected by such cuts.

## The politics of mental health: tensions and solidarities

The current crisis of mental health, alongside the brutal attacks on the benefits of people with mental health problems and rising levels of work-related stress among those who are in employment, sharply pose the question of how we should respond politically. One response from some sections of the movement has been to embrace some form of identity politics based on "reclaiming" Madness (capital M) as a political identity. The editors of *Mad Matters*, for example, a 2013 collection of writings by Canadian activists and academics in the emerging field of Mad Studies suggest:

> In recent years "mad " has flooded back into the language of public culture, and into the work of critical activists and scholars worldwide. For people and organisations engaged in resistance against psychiatry, to take up "madness" is an expressly political act. Following other social movements including queer, black, and fat activism, madness talk and text invert the language of oppression, reclaiming disparaged identities and restoring dignity and pride to difference.[215]

As Cresswell and Spandler note in a discussion of current debates within mental health politics, the argument of these writers and those who share their perspective is not primarily about the need to challenge the stigma attached to mental distress:

> Rather "mental health diagnoses and treatment" are seen as the *direct* source of oppression and therefore *always* productive of sanism.[216]

And "sanism" for those who embrace this perspective is defined as:

> the systematic subjugation of people who have received mental health diagnoses or treatment...sanism may result in various forms of stigma... discrimination and...micro-aggression.[217]

Biomedical psychiatry is therefore indicted by Mad Studies as the principal source of sanism: not only psychiatry, however, but any profession linked to psychiatry such as psychology or social work—what Rose has labelled the "psy" disciplines or more generally "mental health services".

As leading service user activist and academic Peter Beresford notes in his introduction to the Canadian collection, many different perspectives are contained within the field of Mad Studies—there is no single orthodoxy. And in fact many of the contributors have no difficulty in making a link between the struggle against sanism and the struggle against neoliberal capitalism. That said, arguably there are dangers in seeing the source of the difficulties experienced by mental health service users as lying primarily or even solely in psychiatry or in seeing the solution as being in a common Mad identity.

Firstly, very large numbers of people will experience periods of mental distress at some point in their lives. As we saw in Chapter 1, current levels of mental distress, including work-related stress, are at an all-time high. A far smaller number, however, would choose to self-define as "mad", either because the term is generally perceived as too stigmatising or because it does not fit their experience of anxiety, depression or addiction. That suggests that an approach which stresses the commonality of mental distress is likely to have a greater political impact than one which prioritises difference.

Secondly, a majority of people experiencing mental health problems will never encounter a psychiatrist. If they do seek help at all for their distress, it is most likely to be from a counsellor or a GP. Others will suffer in silence, either because they are ashamed of their problem or because no services are available. It is difficult, then, to argue that their problems stem from "psychiatric oppression".

Thirdly, if the origins of psychiatric oppression do lie in the institution and practices of psychiatry rather than in the operations of neoliberal capitalism, then there is an obvious, if drastic, solution. As Bruce Cohen argues in his *Psychiatric Hegemony: a Marxist Theory of Mental Illness* (a text which in fact owes much more to Foucault and labelling theorists than to Marx):

> Despite facing greater levels of social and economic hardship, there is a good reason why people in low-income countries experience less mental illness and have more chance of long-term recovery than their counterparts in higher income countries… Namely they have little or no access to western-trained mental health experts who can readily pathologise their behaviours as signs of mental illness… Thus, despite having some psy-professional friends and colleagues whom I continue to work with on various research projects, I would at this stage be a fool to recommend anything other than the wholesale abolition of their profession.

This is the logical conclusion from my research and theoretical argumentation in this book.[218]

While such calls to close down mental health services may be music to the ears of right wing politicians, were Cohen's arguments to be taken seriously they would add considerably to the misery both of many people with mental health problems (some of whom actually find mental health services helpful) and also the families (and particularly their women members) who would be left to care for their distressed relatives.

Fourthly, basing a movement on a mental health identity suggests that people with mental health problems share a common experience and a common interest which trumps all other factors shaping their lives, including class. It is certainly the case that the stigma surrounding mental health problems affects people in *all* social classes, as do other forms of oppression, and should be challenged wherever it occurs. As I write, for example, Prince Harry, the younger son of the late Princess Diana, has been speaking openly about the mental health problems he has experienced since his mother's untimely death and the need for a more open approach to mental distress. Such openness is to be welcomed. But as the journalist Suzanne Moore commented:

Harry has rightly been praised for talking personally and thus destigmatising mental health issues. This is no doubt excellent. The normalising of mental health problems, which it is estimated will affect a quarter of us at one time or another, is necessary, but so too is funding. Mental health services are in a very poor state and it is almost impossible to get help. Many people in Harry's situation would not get access to counselling and would be offered antidepressants and possibly a short course of cognitive behavioural therapy, as this is considered most cost-effective. In acute cases, people in a state of severe breakdown are now forced to go to hospitals far from their homes because there are no beds to be found nearby. This is a real crisis, and it is more visible by the day on our streets.[219]

Similarly while it is encouraging to see more MPs in the UK prepared to speak out openly about their own mental health problems, in most cases this has not stopped them from voting for the austerity policies which have caused services to be withdrawn or for harsher immigration and asylum laws which destroy the physical and mental health of asylum seekers and refugees. When it comes to a choice, class and politics invariably trump any shared mental health identity.

Finally, given recent research evidence (to be discussed in the next chapter) showing that reactionary ideas about mental distress are not fixed but can be challenged, and given also the extent of mental distress currently in society, the prospects for building a broad, rather than a narrow, movement to challenge the causes of mental distress, defend existing services and put forward alternative visions of the kind of mental health services we need are very good indeed. The final chapter will seek to develop the kind of analysis which can underpin that movement, consider the kind of strategies and aims that might involve and reflect on how a struggle for "more and better" mental health services can relate to the struggle for the kind of society where such services are no longer required.

# 6

# Taking control: alienation and mental health

In this final chapter, I shall consider how Marx's analysis of capitalism and specifically his concept of alienation can contribute to our understanding of the causes of mental distress and how we can challenge these. As a way into this, it may be helpful to begin by contrasting Marx's views with those of Freud.

For Freud, as we saw in Chapter 3, the origins of much unhappiness, neurosis and psychosis were to be found in the repression of our most basic human needs and drives in the interests of "civilisation". He was a sexual reformer who saw much of the sexual repression of his own day as excessive and not conducive to good mental health. Nevertheless, his vision was essentially a pessimistic one. Alex Callinicos has summarised it as follows:

> Freud's general view is that human beings' biological constitution is quite directly responsible for a variety of social phenomena; thus, aggression, whether manifested in personal relationships or on the battlefield, is the death instinct turned outwards. This does not mean he is a biological determinist or an opponent of social reform; but he believes that repression is a necessary condition of the existence of civilisation, which will exert a high price in unhappiness, whatever the form of society.[220]

Marx's starting point, like Freud's, was the given biological constitution of human beings and their requirement, before all else, to meet some basic human needs, notably self-preservation and procreation:

> [W]e must begin by stating the first premise of all human existence and, therefore, of all history, the premise, namely, that men must be in a position to live in order to be able to "make history". But life involves before everything else eating and drinking, a habitation, clothing and many

other things. The first historical act is thus the production of the means to satisfy these needs, the production of material life itself.

Thus social existence precedes social consciousness. Terry Eagleton spells out some similarities here between Marx's materialism and that of Freud:

> [I]t is material need that compels us to produce, and such needs are not primarily a matter of consciousness. Such needs, to be sure, must become aware of themselves if they are to be satisfied. In this sense, thinking is a material necessity. But they germinate in the body rather than the mind. "The need is where we think from", remarks Theodor Adorno in *Negative Dialectics*. Something similar is true for Freud, in whose view the small infant is in the grip of an anarchic set of bodily drives from which the ego is yet to emerge. The mind is belated in relation to the body. When it does appear on the scene, it represses a good many of the forces which went into its making, thrusting them into that non-place we know as the unconscious.[221]

So Marx, like Freud, was a materialist. Human beings were part of nature, driven, like other animals, by basic needs for food, drink, shelter, procreation and so on. But unlike Freud's materialism, which sees human behaviour everywhere as governed to a greater or lesser extent by a small number of relatively unchanging biologically based drives (self-preservation, sexuality, the death drive) and the inevitable conflict between these and society, Marx's materialism is a profoundly *historical* materialism at the heart of which is his particular view of human nature.

Marx rejected popular notions of human nature which saw it as fixed, static and unchanging and which often simply reflected the dominant values of the society of the day, such as egoism, greed or aggression.

By contrast, he stressed the huge variability of human behaviour across different cultures and different historical epochs and that what is called "human nature" or the "human essence" is in reality an embodiment and reflection of the specific values and practices of particular societies:

> [T]he human essence is no abstraction inherent in each single individual. In its reality it is the ensemble of the social relations.[222]

It would be wrong to conclude from this, however, that Marx had no concept of human nature or that it played no role in his theoretical schema. Rather, he distinguished between what he called "human nature in general" and "human nature as historically modified in each epoch".[223] What, then, for Marx characterised "human nature in general"? What was it that made us distinctively human?

The earliest statement of Marx's views on human nature (and indeed, of the materialist conception of history) are to be found in *The German Ideology*, written in 1845:

> Men can be distinguished from animals by consciousness, by religion or anything else you like. They themselves begin to distinguish themselves from animals as soon as they begin to produce their means of subsistence, a step which is conditioned by their physical organisation. By producing their means of subsistence men are indirectly producing their actual material life.[224]

For Marx, three consequences flow from this distinctly human attribute. First, by "producing their means of subsistence", through, for example, the creation of weapons for hunting, tools for farming, pots for carrying food, the use of fire, the invention of the wheel and so on, human beings transform the world in which they live in a way that no other animals can. As Marx acknowledged in *The Communist Manifesto*, the speed and scale of that transformation reached new heights with the development of capitalism.

Second, this transformation did not involve only technological change but also changes in social relations within society. For reasons explored by Marx, and more fully later by Engels, these changes led eventually—and in a process which was far from automatic or inevitable—to the development of class societies in which a small minority of people controlled the social surplus and exploited and oppressed a much bigger group, be they slaves, serfs or proletarians, who produced the wealth in society. In other words, the world which human beings had created began in turn to shape and dominate their lives, a process which has reached both its highest and its lowest point in our own epoch, the Anthropocene, where man-made climate change threatens the very existence of life on earth.[225]

The third aspect of our specifically human nature identified by Marx has particular relevance for our understanding of mental health.

For in acting upon the world in a purposeful way, we also change ourselves, discover new potentialities, create new needs. As Terry Eagleton observes:

> In his early writings, Marx speaks of what he calls "species being", which is really a materialist version of human nature. Because of the nature of our material bodies, we are needy, labouring, sociable, sexual, communicative, self-expressive animals who need one another to survive, but who come to find a fulfilment in that companionship over and above its social usefulness... Because we are labouring, desiring, linguistic creatures, we are able to transform ourselves at the same time. Change in other words, is not the opposite of human nature; it is possible because of the creative, open-ended, unfinished beings we are.[226]

Nor was that view of human nature some youthful, romantic residue from Marx's early Hegelian period. In a discussion of the labour process some 30 years later in *Capital*, he wrote:

> Labour is, first of all, a process between man and nature, a process by which man, through his own actions, mediates, regulates and controls the metabolism between himself and nature... Through this movement he acts upon external nature and changes it, and in this way he simultaneously changes his own nature. He develops the potentialities slumbering within nature, and subjects the play of its forces to his own sovereign power. We are not dealing here with those first instinctive forms of labour which remain on the animal level. An immense interval of time separates the state of things in which a man brings his labour-power to market for sale as a commodity from the situation in which human labour had not yet cast off its first instinctive form. We presuppose labour in a form in which it is an exclusively human characteristic.[227]

For Marx, then, it is what John Rees calls "the most fundamental of all human attributes, the ability consciously to control your own labour" that makes us human.[228] It is precisely this open-endedness, this potential for development, that makes us human, is our "essence"; as Marx argued, "freedom is so much the essence of man that even its opponents realise it in that they fight its reality".[229] But as he showed in his re-working of Hegel's concept of alienation, it is precisely that attribute and that potential which is most comprehensively denied by the economic system in which we live—capitalism. As Rees comments:

The paradox is that just as society developed a powerful enough productive engine to escape the misery, disease and early death of capitalism, just as the wealth of society became great enough to provide for all, human beings' ability to control society was abolished by the very structure that produced the wealth.[230]

What, then, are the consequences of that lack of control for our mental health? Answering that question requires us to look more closely at Marx's theory of alienation.

## Alienation and mental distress

For Marx, capitalism was a system characterised by two great divides. The first divide was between that tiny minority of people who owned the means of production—the ruling class—and the great mass of people who could only live by selling their labour power, their ability to work—the working class.

The second divide was between the different competing units of capital whose survival and growth depended on their ability to make sufficient profits, based on the exploitation of their workforce. For Marx, this was not a question of "good" employers or "bad" employers. The logic of the system, he argued, required capitalists (and the governments which represented them) to do whatever was necessary to compete effectively in the marketplace, whether that be cutting wages, increasing the working day, or cutting back on welfare spending. This is particularly evident in a period like the present where the recovery from the Great Crash of 2008 has been very weak. As Chris Harman comments:

> Capital is not then defined just by exploitation (which occurred in many precapitalist societies) but by its necessary drive to self-expansion. The motivation for production and exchange is increasing the amount of value in the hands of the capitalist firm... So the system is not just a system of commodity production; it is also a system of competitive accumulation. This creates limits to the action possible not only for workers, but also for capitalists... They can choose to exploit their workers in one way rather than another. But they cannot choose not to exploit their workers at all, or even to exploit them less than other capitalists do—unless they want to go bust. They themselves are subject to

a system which pursues its reckless course whatever the feelings of human beings.[231]

Capitalism, then, is a system out of the control both of those who claim to manage it and of those who create its wealth. But the effects of that loss of control are far more severe for the exploited class than for those who run the system. Alienation, argues Bertell Ollman,

> is the intellectual construct in which Marx displays the devastating effects of capitalist production on human beings, on their physical and mental states, and on the social processes of which they are a part.[232]

We have discussed above one feature of that alienation—namely, the denial by capitalism of our specifically human ability to perform conscious labour. Marx identifies three further aspects of alienation.[233]

Firstly, under capitalism the worker has no control over *what* is produced—the product of his or her labour. This belongs to, and is disposed of, by the employer. In previous societies, people used their creative abilities to produce goods which they would consume, exchange or sell. By contrast, under capitalism, many workers will often be unable to purchase the item that they have produced, be it a pair of designer jeans, a personal computer or a new car.

Secondly, there is a loss of control over the labour process itself. As we have seen above, Marx conceives of work not in the narrow sense of paid labour but rather as creative, conscious activity. Under capitalism, however, not only the goal and the end product of such activity are determined by others, but so too is the work process. This means that such work is usually experienced as anything but fulfilling. In Marx's own words:

> labour is external to the worker ie does not belong to his essential being; that he therefore does not confirm himself in his work, but denies himself, feels miserable and not happy, does not develop free mental and physical energy, but mortifies his flesh and ruins his mind. Hence the worker feels himself only when he is not working; when he is working he does not feel himself. He is at home when he is not working, and not at home when he is working. His labour is therefore not voluntary but forced, it is forced labour. It is therefore not the satisfaction of a need but a mere means to satisfy needs outside itself. Its alien character is clearly demonstrated by the fact that

as soon as no physical or other compulsion exists it is shunned like the plague.[234]

The description fits perfectly the common experience of work today. In factories, offices, telephone call centres, fast food outlets, schools, hospitals, social work departments and even universities, those who actually perform the labour find their "freedom" restricted, the controls pervasive and the regime tightening.

The third aspect of alienation discussed by Marx is alienation from our fellow human beings. Most obviously, there is the alienation between those who own or control the means of production and those whom they exploit. The competition that drives capitalism leaves little room for feelings of human solidarity or collective interest between capitalist and capitalist on the one hand, and between capitalist and worker on the other. But, as Bertell Ollman argues, alienation also shapes relations between the worker and his or her fellow workers:

> Competition may thus be viewed as the activity which produces class. Throughout society, calculator meets calculator in the never-ending battle of who can get the most out of whom. "Mutual exploitation" is the rule. Other people are mere objects of use; their wishes and feelings are never considered, cannot be on pain of extinction. A lapse into kindness for those who have their own knives poised can be fatal. In this situation, hearts are opened only to absolute losers; charity becomes the only form of giving.[235]

And so the very nature of capitalism divides workers. Workers' labour power becomes a mere commodity sold on the labour market. Here, they are forced to compete against each other for jobs and scarce resources and this creates the material conditions that breed the major divisions—such as racism, sexism and homophobia—that fracture modern life. No less importantly—and of great concern to Marx—that lack of control has profound implications for workers' physical and mental health.

So, for example, the Whitehall studies of civil servants carried out over many years by Michael Marmot and his colleagues found a strong association between grade levels of civil servant employment and mortality rates from a range of causes: the lower the grade, the higher the mortality rate. Men in the lowest grade (for example messengers and doorkeepers) had a mortality rate three times higher than that of men in the highest grade (administrators). Commenting on these studies in *The Spirit Level*, Wilkinson and Pickett note:

> Of all the factors that the Whitehall researchers have studied over the years, job stress and people's sense of control seem to make the most difference.[236]

They go on to suggest that the central issue here is inequality and low social status and the associated feeling of inferiority that comes with it. As their book demonstrates, inequality does indeed matter. However, it is not just inequality or low status that causes these health problems. Rather, as Dan Swain argues:

> The roots of these problems are to be found in the way in which our social and working lives are organised, and that is first and foremost defined by a lack of control. It is not just the gap between the richest and the poorest but the divisions between bosses and workers that affects our health and well-being. Inequality is likely to be an indicator of class position and alienation—those with least control over their work are also likely to be the least paid and vice versa—but it is not the root cause.[237]

That loss of control begins in the workplace but shapes every aspect of life under capitalism, whether economic, political, social or emotional. As Jimmy Reid, then a member of the British Communist Party and a leader of the historic Upper Clyde Shipbuilders work-in in Clydebank, spelled out in his 1972 Rectorial Address at Glasgow University:

> Alienation is the precise and correctly applied word for describing the major social problem in Britain today... Let me right at the outset define what I mean by alienation. It is the cry of men who feel themselves the victims of blind economic forces beyond their control. It is the frustration of ordinary people excluded from the processes of decision making. The feeling of despair and hopelessness that pervades people who feel with justification that they have no real say in shaping or determining their own destinies.[238]

That denial of people's capacity to shape their own lives and the frustration and despair to which it gives rise underlies much of the violence and aggression that mars lives and communities under capitalism. Following the riots which broke out in several English cities in the mid-1990s, for example, the journalist Nick Davies interviewed dozens of the young men who had been involved. What he found, as he reported in his book *Dark Heart*, was that:

> [T]hey suffered not only a lack of material things but also a deep lack of opportunity to do anything about it. There were many people here who would never escape and who knew that to be the fact of their lives: they felt a deep despair which occasionally erupted in aggression and crime.[239]

Alongside that powerlessness was a denial of their creative ability, of what, in Marx's view, makes us human:

> They all had their own dreams, most of them very mundane. They wanted to go to college, get a job or simply to have something to do all day. In real life, as they readily described, there were only two things to do—thieving and twocking [stealing cars]. They wanted much more. Their lives refused to let them have it, so they became frustrated and hopeless and bitterly angry. And they fought their war against the law with a furious rage.[240]

The concept of alienation is also crucial in helping us make sense of mental distress. Firstly, as the Whitehall study referred to above shows, the experience of feeling powerless can itself contribute directly to physical and mental problems, including depression and anxiety. Powerlessness, in other words, makes you ill. Reference was made in Chapter 1 to the correlation between the decline in the number of days "lost" in strikes since the 1980s and the huge rise since then in work-related stress which now accounts for 50 percent of all sickness absences. Where workers lack the confidence or the organisation to express their grievances collectively, then frustration and anger are individualised and turned against the self. There is a strong connection, in other words, between the level of class struggle and levels of mental health problems in society.

Secondly, a loss of control is a characteristic feature of many forms of mental distress. According to social psychiatrist Tom Burns:

> Central to psychiatry's understanding of mental illness is a judgement that patients have become somehow "different" and that this is not under their control... Mental illness includes a sense of change, of

"alienation" from the normal self and a sense of a lack of control over that change.[241]

So for example, the lives of people diagnosed as schizophrenic will often be dominated by the voices that they hear; for those with depression or anxiety, by intense, frightening or painful feelings that do not seem appropriate to the actual situation that they face; and for those with eating disorders or phobias, by food or by fears which shape every aspect of their lives. In each case, there is a loss of freedom or control due to feelings or voices which in reality belong to the individual affected but which are experienced as alien to them.

Thirdly, the relations between people with mental health problems and those responsible for their care have often been characterised by the most extreme powerlessness on one side and on the other a degree of control—both legal and ideological—over body and mind which goes beyond that permitted in any other area of adult social care or medicine. Service users in Scotland stressed the disempowering effects of such a model:

> That's the model that the users' movement was formed to oppose. That's what creates mental illness. Losing sight of personal worth, taking away personal autonomy—that makes mental health problems worse. That model belittles and infantilises.[242]

## What is to be done?

Our understanding of the roots of mental distress will shape our view of the kind of services we need to fight for in the here and now as well as pointing to the kind of world in which there would be much less emotional and psychological misery. In terms of the first point, Peter Kinderman has argued that:

> Services planned on the basis of a psycho-social model would offer a very radical alternative. Instead of seeing care for people with mental health problems as a specialist branch of medicine, with links to social care, we would see such support as essentially part of social provision, with specialist input from our medical colleagues. In such a world, people would default to a psychosocial explanatory model and the disease model of mental disorder would be redundant.[243]

Key elements of that model, Kinderman suggests, would include services based on the premise that the origins of mental distress are largely social—in other words, a social model of mental distress; services based on people's own descriptions of their problems rather than on psychiatric diagnoses; greatly reduced, and more pragmatic, use of medication; services individualised to people's needs; and much less use of coercion.

Much of what Kinderman proposes fits with what activists in the mental health service user movement have been arguing for since the movement began in the 1970s. In particular, the demand for greater choice and control, both over the type of services on offer and over other aspects of their lives, is a key one, scarcely surprising given the denial of self-determination which many people with mental health problems have historically experienced. The demand of the wider disability movement for independent living as well as the slogan of "nothing about us without us" applics no less to mental health service users.

Such progressive visions, however, also need to be located in a concrete political context. For a feature of neoliberal ideology over the past three decades has been its capacity to appropriate progressive-sounding ideas and language (such as choice, control and empowerment) and utilise them for less than progressive ends. Discussing the experience of the disability movement in the UK, disability writer and activist Jenny Morris highlights the dangers that can arise:

> One key example of past successes in finding opportunities within prevailing political agendas concerns the campaign for direct payments. The resulting legislation, passed by a Conservative government in 1996, fitted in with an agenda which sought the privatisation of services and an undermining of public sector trade unions. While disabled people's organisations did not support such policies, we did—when making the case for direct payments—use language which fitted well with the individualist political framework which was becoming more and more dominant. Thus we emphasised disabled people's rights to autonomy and self-determination, which resonated with the Conservative government's agenda; and drew attention to the way a lack of choice and control could undermine human rights, which then fitted well with New Labour's agenda. My concern is that—in engaging with the dominant policy agendas—we have lost touch with more fundamental issues concerning the welfare state, and that we have, unintentionally,

contributed towards a steady undermining of collective responsibility and redistribution. From my perspective, this matters because I do not believe that the alternative—a small state and a market of private providers—will deliver the opportunities and quality of life which disabled people should expect in the twenty-first century.[244]

The same point can be made in respect of what is currently one of the most influential notions in UK mental health policy: recovery. In itself, the concept of recovery is a progressive one and one which emerged in the first instance from the experience of service users. A definition is provided by the Scottish Recovery Network:

> Recovery is being able to live a meaningful and satisfying life, as defined by each person, in the presence of absence of symptoms. It is about having control over and input into your own life. Each individual's recovery, like his or her experience of mental health problems or illness, is a unique and deeply personal process.[245]

For Patricia Deegan, a US mental health activist and one of the first people to promote the concept:

> The concept of recovery differs from that of rehabilitation in as much as it emphasises that people are responsible for their own lives and that we can take a stand toward our disability and what is distressing to us. We need not be passive victims. We need not be "afflicted". We can become responsible agents in our own recovery process.[246]

This emphasis on people finding their own ways through mental distress (with or without the use of medication) on the one hand and the rejection of the pessimism and despair often associated with bio-medical models on the other can sound—and often is—inspiring. At the same time, however, it can also fit with a view of "independence" shaped by neoliberalism as meaning individual responsibility and a withdrawal of properly funded services and supports. That is a dangerous message to send out at a time when mental health services in the UK, both in the voluntary sector and in the NHS, are being slashed as part of the austerity policies imposed by successive right wing governments. As the campaigning organisation Recovery in the Bin has argued in its *Twenty Principles of Recovery*:

We believe that the concept of "recovery" has been colonised by mental health services, commissioners and policy makers. We believe the growing development of this form of the "Recovery Model" is a symptom of neoliberalism, and that capitalism is at the root of the crisis! Many of us will never be able to "recover" living under these intolerable social and economic conditions, due to the effects of circumstances such as poor housing, poverty, stigma, racism, sexism, unreasonable work expectations, and countless other barriers.[247]

Similarly, the definition of independent living put forward by the Independent Living Movement in Scotland makes the point that independence is conditional on social supports being in place:

Independent living means all disabled people having the same freedom, choice, dignity and control as other citizens at home, at work and in the community. It does not necessarily mean living by yourself or fending for yourself. It means rights to practical assistance and support to participate in society and live an ordinary life.[248]

In practice, that points to the need to fight to protect the mental health services we do have (including emergency psychiatric beds so that people do not have to travel hundreds of miles in a crisis in order to find a bed) while also fighting for the kind of less medicalised services which service users have now been demanding (and sometimes achieving) for almost four decades.

Closing her account of her experience as an in-patient in the late 1980s in Friern Barnet hospital in London (long closed and, like so many former psychiatric hospitals, now turned into luxury flats), the writer and historian Barbara Taylor poses the question of how different her experience would be were she to have a psychotic breakdown today:

The mental health system I entered in the 1980s was deeply flawed, but at least it recognised needs—for ongoing care, for asylum, for someone to rely upon when self-reliance is no option—that the present system pretends do not exist, offering in their stead individualist pieties that are a mockery of people's sufferings. The story of the Asylum Age is not a happy one. But if the death of the asylum means the demise of effective and humane mental health care, then this will be more than a bad ending to the story: it will be a tragedy.[249]

## Conclusion: taking control

In June 2017, the *Guardian* newspaper reported that prescriptions for 64.7 million items of antidepressants were dispensed in England in 2016—a staggering 108.5 percent increase on the 31 million antidepressants dispensed ten years earlier and an all time high.[250] Less than two weeks earlier, the same newspaper reported that tens of thousands of young people in England, including children as young as six, were being prescribed antidepressants by their doctors. As the journalist commented, "misery appears to be escalating at an alarming scale".

In this connection it is worth repeating the conclusion, cited in Chapter 1, of Brown and Harris's classic research study of depression in women published in 1978:

> While we see sadness, unhappiness and grief as inevitable in all societies we do not believe this is true of clinical depression.[251]

In other words, to summarise the central message of this book, there is nothing "natural" about emotional misery on this scale. There is no evidence to show it is the product of diseased brains or faulty genes. There is, however, considerable evidence to show that it is the logical outcome of extreme levels of inequality which leave those at the bottom of the hierarchy feeling like useless failures—"losers" in the language of the odious Donald J Trump.

It is the predictable consequence of an individualist ideology where the insistence that "there is no such thing as society" alongside draconian cuts to public services and social spaces has created an epidemic of loneliness and social isolation that fuels depression and anxiety. And it is the inevitable consequence of a relentless drive for increased productivity and profitability that drives young workers in Foxcom factories in China to suicide and their Western counterparts to visit their GPs in droves with work-related stress as they struggle to survive on zero-hours contracts. On this last point, it would be hard to improve on the bitter sarcasm of the young Marx in 1844:

> Time for education, for intellectual development, for the fulfilment of social functions, for social intercourse, for the free play of the vital forces of his body and his mind, even the rest time of Sunday (and that in a country of Sabbatarians!)—what foolishness!... Capital asks no questions about the length of life of labour power. What interests it is

purely and simply the maximum of labour power that can be set in motion in a working day. It attains this objective by shortening the life of labour power, in the same way as a greedy farmer snatches more produce from the soil by robbing it of its fertility.[252]

But there is another side to this grim picture. In part because people with mental health problems are no longer shut away in distant asylums; in part because mental distress is now so widespread; and in part because of the many struggles in recent years by mental health service users, trade unionists and campaigning organisations against stigma and for more and better services, there has been a sea-change in attitudes towards people with mental health problems.

The Time to Change project has been carrying out annual large-scale surveys of attitudes towards mental illness in the UK since 1994. Its *Attitudes to Mental Illness* 2013 found that attitudes towards people with mental illness are more favourable in 2013 than they were in 2008. So, for example, there has been a decline in the proportions agreeing that:

- "Anyone with a history of mental problems should be excluded from public office", from 21 percent in 2008 to 13 percent in 2013, with a significant difference also in the results between 2012 (18 percent) and 2013
- "It is frightening to think of people with mental problems living in residential neighbourhoods", from 16 percent to 10 percent, with a significant difference also in the results between 2012 (13 percent) and 2013
- "I would not want to live next door to someone who has been mentally ill", from 12 percent to 8 percent
- "People with mental illness are a burden on society", from 7 percent to 5 percent, with a significant difference also in the results between 2012 (7 percent) and 2013
- "Locating mental health facilities in a residential area downgrades the neighbourhood", from 20 percent to 16 percent.

The report's authors also found that understanding and tolerance of mental illness had increased since 2008, although, because the level of tolerance was already high in 2008, the increases were quite small. There has been a statistically significant increase in the proportion who said that they agreed with the statements:

- "We need to adopt a far more tolerant attitude toward people with mental illness in our society", from 83 percent in 2008 to 89 percent in 2013
- "As far as possible, mental health services should be provided through community-based facilities", from 72 percent to 77 percent
- "People with mental illness have for too long been the subject of ridicule", from 75 percent to 79 percent
- "We have a responsibility to provide the best possible care for people with mental illness", from 89 percent to 93 percent, and
- "Virtually anyone can become mentally ill" from 89 percent to 92 percent

The report's overall finding was that

Analysis of summary scores across all of the community attitudes to mental illness (CAMI) statements confirmed that overall attitudes towards mental illness have become more favourable since 2008, with a significant increase also since 2012.[253]

That degree of understanding and support provides a strong basis for defending services and building solidarity with people experiencing mental health problems. In fact, a positive feature of recent years has been precisely the high level of joint action between service user organisations; public sector trade unions, such as UNISON and PCS; and campaigning groups, such as the Social Work Action Network and Psychologists against Austerity, to challenge the austerity policies of the Coalition and Conservative governments.

In conclusion, however, one factor more than any other would contribute to a real improvement in the mental health of the vast majority of people in Britain and elsewhere. In their study of the rise of the trade union Solidarity in Poland in the early 1980s, Colin Barker and Kara Weber cite a newspaper report which suggested that as the workers' movement there grew in confidence and organisation and as the regime's supporters became more afraid that they were losing their grip on power, the hospitals emptied of workers who wanted to be part of the struggle and began to fill up instead with the old Communist Party bureaucrats.[254] The story may be apocryphal but it highlights the point that when working class people gain a sense of their collective power, it can have a very positive effect on their health. Similarly, in his study of the Egyptian Revolution of 2011, Jack Shenker writes:

> That new-found sense of agency, of an ability to shape things around you in ways you never knew existed—that gave me my definition of revolution: not a time-bound occurrence, nor a shuffle of rules and faces up top, but rather a state of mind. It felt as if nothing could ever be the same again.[255]

Since then, of course, a counter-revolution has taken place in Egypt, while in Britain and other European countries the level of class struggle remains very low. There are signs, however, that that may be beginning to change. It is still very early days but if the widespread popular desire for a different world reflected during 2016 and 2017 in electoral support for the left wing policies of Jeremy Corbyn in Britain, for Bernie Sanders in the USA and for Jean-Luc Melenchon in France can be translated in the coming months and years into mass struggles in which people begin once more to gain a sense of their own power, then the prospects for our collective mental health could be very much better than they are at present.

In this situation, the priority for all of us who wish to improve our own mental health and the mental health of those around us is both to participate in collective struggles for more and better mental health services—to support the shift back "from worry lines to picket lines"— and also to fight for a world where such services are no longer required.

# Bibliography

Adams, T, "Is there too much stress on stress?", *Guardian*, 14 February 2016, theguardian.com/society/2016/feb/14/workplace-stress-hans-selye

Allen, G, *Early Intervention: Smart Investment, Massive Savings, Independent Report*, HM Government, 2011

Appignanesi, L, *Mad, Bad and Sad: A History of Women and the Mind Doctors from 1800 to the Present*, London, Virago, 2008

Barker C, and Weber, K, "Solidarnosc: from Gdansk to Military Repression", *International Socialism* 15 (special issue), 1982

Benjamin, W, *Selected Writings, Volume 4, 1938-40*, Harvard University Press, 2003

Bentall, R, *Madness Explained: Psychosis and Human Nature*, London, Penguin, 2003

Bentall, R, *Doctoring the Mind: Why Psychiatric Treatments Fail*, London, Penguin, 2010

Bentall, R, "Mental illness is the result of misery, yet still we stigmatise it", *Guardian*, 26 February 2016

Bentall, R, "Has the pandemic really caused a 'tsunami' of mental health problems?", *Guardian*, 9 February 2021, www.theguardian.com/commentisfree/2021/feb/09/pandemic-mental-health-problems-research-coronavirus

Beresford, P "From psycho-politics to mad studies: learning from the legacy of Peter Sedgwick", *Critical and Radical Social Work*, 4 (3), 2016, pp343-355

Blackledge, P, *Marxism and Ethics*, State University of New York Press, 2012

Booth, R, "Government 'to cut £250m from social care workforce funding' in England", *Guardian*, 17 March 2023, www.theguardian.com/society/2023/mar/17/government-to-cut-250m-from-social-care-workforce-funding-in-england-report-says/

Boyle, M and L Johnstone, *A Straight Talking Introduction to the Power Threat Meaning Framework: an Alternative to Psychiatric Diagnosis*, London, PCCS Books, 2020

Bracken, P, Thomas, P and Timimi, S, "Psychiatry beyond the current paradigm", *British Journal of Psychiatry*, 2012, 201:430-434

Branfield, F and Beresford, P, *Making User Involvement Work: Supporting Service User Networking and Knowledge*, York, Joseph Rowntree Foundation, 2006

Brown, G and Harris, T, *Social Origins of Depression: a Study of Psychiatric Disorder in Women*, London, Tavistock Publications, 1978

Brown, G, Birley, J, and Wing, J, "Influence of family life on the course of schizophrenic disorder: a replication", *British Journal of Psychiatry*, 1972, 121, 241-258

Burns, T, *Our Necessary Shadow: The Nature and Meaning of Psychiatry*, London, Allen Lane, 2013

Burns, T and J Foot, *Basaglia's International Legacy: From Asylums to Community*, Oxford University Press, 2020.

Callinicos, A, *Social Theory: A Historical Introduction*, London, Polity, 1999

Callinicos, A, *The New Age of Catastrophe*, Cambridge, London, Polity, 2023

Campbell, D, "Millions with mental health needs not seeking NHS help, watchdog says", *Guardian*, 9 February 2023, www.theguardian.com/society/2023/feb/09/millions-with-mental-health-needs-not-seeking-nhs-help-watchdog-says/

Campbell, P, "The history of the user movement in the United Kingdom" in Heller, T, Reynolds, J, Gomm, R, Musten, R, and Pattison, T (eds), *Mental Health Matters*, Basingstoke, Macmillan, 1996

Choonara, J, "The British Labour Movements Halting Recovery", *International Socialism* 178, spring 2023, www.isj.org.uk/halting-recovery/

Cohen, B M Z, *Psychiatric Hegemony: a Marxist Theory of Mental Illness*, Palgrave Macmillan, 2017

Collier, A, "Lacan, psychoanalysis and the Left", *International Socialism* 7 (Winter 1989), pp51-71

Conn, D, "Revealed: Tory peer Michelle Mone secretly received £29m from 'VIP lane' PPE firm", *Guardian*, 23 November, www.theguardian.com/uk-news/2022/nov/23/revealed-tory-peer-michelle-mone-secretly-received-29m-from-vip-lane-ppe-firm

Cooper, D (ed), *The Dialectics of Liberation*, London, Verso, 1968/2015

Cresswell, M and Spandler, H, "Solidarities and tensions in mental health politics: Mad Studies and Psychopolitics", *Critical and Radical Social Work*, 2016, 4:3, pp357-373

Davies, J, *Cracked: Why Psychiatry is Doing More Harm Than Good*, Iconbooks, 2014

Davies, J, *Sedated: How Modern Capitalism Created Our Mental Health Crisis*, London, Atlantic Books, 2022

Davis, M, *The Monster Enters: Covid-19, the Avian Flu and the Plagues of Capitalism*, London, Verso, 2020

Davis, N and Duncan, P, "Electroconvulsive therapy on the rise again in England", *Guardian*, 17 April 2017

Davies, N, *Dark Heart*, London, Vintage, 1998

Davies, W, *The Happiness Industry*, London, Verso, 2013

de Aguiar, LJP, MIB Bellini and APV Ronsani, "Brazilian psychiatric reform: advances and constraints", *Critical and Radical Social Work*, March 2022, pp93-108.

Deegan, P, "Recovery and the Conspiracy of Hope", Conference presentation, 1996, patdeegan.com/pat-deegan/lectures/conspiracy-of-hope

Deutscher, I, *The Prophet Unarmed*, Oxford, Oxford University Press, 1970

Deutscher, I, *The Prophet Outcast*, Oxford, Oxford University Press, 1970

Devlin, H, "Living near heavy traffic increases risk of dementia, say scientists', *Guardian*, 5 January 2017, theguardian.com/society/2017/jan/04/living-near-heavy-traffic-increases-dementia-risk-say-scientists

Dillon, J, Johnstone, L and Longden, E, "Trauma, Dissociation, Attachment and Neuroscience: A New Paradigm for Understanding Severe Mental Distress" in Speed, E, Moncrieff, J and Rapley M (eds), *De-medicalizing Misery II*, 2014

Durkheim, E, *Suicide: A Study in Sociology*, 2013, snowballpublishing.com

Eagleton, T, *Trouble with Strangers: A Study of Ethics*, Chichester, Wiley-Blackwell, 2009

Eagleton, T, *Why Marx was Right*, Yale University Press, 2011

Eagleton, T, *Materialism*, New Haven and London, Yale University Press, 2016

Engels, F, *The Condition of the Working-Class in England*, London, Lawrence and Wishart, 1844/1973

Fee E and Brown T M, "Freeing the Insane", *American Journal of Public Health*, October 2006; 96(10): 1743

Ferguson, I, "The Potential and Limits of Mental Health Service User Involvement", unpublished PhD Thesis, University of Glasgow, 1999

Ferguson, I, " Identity politics or class struggle? The case of the mental health users' movement" in Lavalette, M and Mooney, G (eds), *Class Struggle and Social Welfare*, 2000, London: Routledge, pp228-249

Ferguson, I, "Neoliberalism, happiness and

well-being", *International Socialism* 117, 2007, pp87-121

Ferguson, I, "Between Marx and Freud: Erich Fromm Revisited", *International Socialism* 149, 2016, pp151-174

Ferguson, I and Lavalette, M, "Beyond Power Discourse: Alienation and Social Work", *The British Journal of Social Work*, vol 34, issue 3, 1, 2004, pp297-312

Ferguson, I, Petrie, M and Stalker, K, *Developing Accessible Services for Homeless People with Severe Mental Distress and Behavioural Difficulties*, University of Stirling, 2005

Ferguson, I, "Capitalism, Coronavirus and Mental Distress", *International Socialism* 168, autumn 2020, pp83-107, www.isj.org.uk/coronavirus-mental-distress/

Filer, N, *The Heartland: Finding and Losing Schizophrenia,* London, Faber and Faber, 2019

Foot, J, *The Man who Closed the Asylums: Franco Basaglia and the Revolution in Mental Health Care*, London, Verso, 2015

Forgacs, D, (ed), *The Antonio Gramsci Reader*, London, Lawrence and Wishart, 1999

Fotheringham, B, D Sherry and C Bryce (eds) *Breaking Up the British State: Scotland, Independence and Socialism,* London, Bookmarks, 2021.

Foucault, M, *Madness and Civilization: A History of Insanity in the Age of Reason*, London, Routledge, 2001

Freud, S, "The Question of a Weltanschauung" in Gay P (ed), *The Freud Reader*, London, Vintage Books, 1995

Fromm, E, *Marx's Concept of Man*, Unger Press, 1966

Frosh, S, *A Brief Introduction to Psychoanalytic Theory*, Basingstoke, Palgrave Macmillan, 2012

Geras, N, *Marxism and Human Nature: Refutation of a Legend*, London, Verso, 1983/2016

Greenberg, G, *The Book of Woe: the DSM and the Unmaking of Psychiatry*, Scribe UK, 2013

Hall, R, "'Buckling' NHS fails to treat 250,000 children with mental health problems", *Guardian*, 16 April 2023, www.theguardian.com/education/2023/apr/16/buckling-nhs-fails-to-treat-250000-children-with-mental-health-problems/

Harman, C, *The Fire Last Time: 1968 and After*, London, Bookmarks, 1988

Harman, C, "Gramsci, the Prison Notebooks and philosophy", *International Socialism* 114, 2007, isj.org.uk/gramsci-the-prison-notebooks-and-philosophy/

Harman, C, *Zombie Capitalism*, London, Bookmarks, 2009

Harris, J and White, V, *Oxford Dictionary of Social Work and Social Care*, Oxford University Press, 2013

Health and Safety Executive, 2016, hse.gov.uk/statistics/causdis/stress/

Henley, J, "Recessions can hurt but austerity kills', *Guardian*, 15 May 2013 theguardian.com/society/2013/may/15/recessions-hurt-but-austerity-kills

Herzog, D, *Cold War Freud: Psychoanalysis in an Age of Catastrophes*, Cambridge, Cambridge University Press, 2017

Hollander, N, *Love in a Time of Hate: Liberation Psychology in Latin America*, New Jersey, Brunswick Press, 1997

Jacoby, R, *The Repression of Psychoanalysis: Otto Fenichel and the Political Freudians*, Chicago, University of Chicago Press, 1986

Kimber, C, "'The strike is liberating'—day 11 of French revolt", *Socialist Worker*, 6 April 2023, www.socialistworker.co.uk/international/the-strike-is-liberating-day-11-of-french-revolt/

Kinderman, P, "A Manifesto for Psychological Health and Wellbeing" in J Davies (ed) *The Sedated Society: The Causes and Harms of our Psychiatric Drug Epidemic*, Basingstoke, Palgrave Macmillan, 2017

King's Fund, *Mental Health Under Pressure*, 2015, kingsfund.org.uk/sites/default/files/field/field_publication_file/mental-health-under-pressure-nov15_0.pdf

Knapp, M, "Mental health in an age of austerity", *Evidence-Based Mental*

*Health Notebook*, 2012, ebmh.bmj.com/content/15/3/54

Kotowicz, Z, *R D Laing and the Paths of Anti-Psychiatry*, London, Routledge, 1997

Van der Kolk, B, *The Body Keeps the Score: Mind, Body and Brain in the Transformation of Trauma*, London, Penguin, 2014

Kimber, C, "Why did Labour Lose?", *International Socialism* 166, spring 2020, isj.org.uk/why-did-labour-lose/

Kovel, J, *A Complete Guide to Therapy: From Psychoanalysis to Behaviour Modification*, Harmondsworth, Penguin, 1978

Laing, R D, *The Divided Self*, London, Pelican, 1960/1965

Laing, R D, and Esterson, A, *Sanity, Madness and the Family*, 2nd ed, London, Pelican, 1969

Laing, R D, *The Politics of Experience*, London, Pelican, 1967

Laing, R D, *Wisdom, Madness and Folly: The Making of a Psychiatrist*, Edinburgh, Canongate Classics, 2001

Lorenz, W, *Social Work in a Changing Europe*, London, Routledge, 1994

Lott, T, "What does depression feel like? Trust me, you really don't want to know", *Guardian*, 19 April 2016, theguardian.com/commentisfree/2016/apr/19/depression-awareness-mental-illness-feel-like

Marx, K, "Economic and Philosophical Manuscripts" in K Marx, *Early Writings*, Harmondsworth, Penguin, 1844/1975

Marx, K, *Theses on Feuerbach*, 1845, marxists.org/archive/marx/works/1845/theses/theses.htm

Marx, K, *Capital*, vol 1, London, Penguin, 1976

Marx, K and Engels, F, *The German Ideology*, 1846, marxists.org/archive/marx/works/1845/german-ideology/ch01a.htm

Masson, J, *The Assault on Truth: Freud's Suppression of the Seduction Theory*, Pocket Books, 1998

Mental Health Foundation, *Fundamental Facts about Mental Health*, London:

Mental Health Foundation, 2016

Mental Health Foundation, *Surviving or Thriving? The State of the UK's Mental Health*, London, 2017

Mental Health Foundation, *Fundamental Facts about Mental Health 2016*, London

Menzies, R, LeFrancois, B A and Reaume, G, "Introducing Mad Studies" in LeFrancois, B A, Menzies, R and Reaume, G (eds), *Mad Matters: a Critical Reader in Canadian Mad Studies*, Toronto: Canadian Scholars Press, 2013

Miller, M, *Freud and the Bolsheviks*, New Haven and London, Yale University Press, 1998

Mills, C Wright, *The Sociological Imagination*, USA, Oxford University Press, 1959/2000

Mitchell, J, *Psychoanalysis and Feminism*, London, Penguin, 1974

Molyneux, J, "What is the Real Marxist Tradition?", *International Socialism*, July 1983 marxists.org/history/etol/writers/molyneux/1983/07/tradition.htm

Moore, S, "The lesson of Prince Harry's grief? We need mental health services for all", *Guardian*, 17 April 2017

Morris, J, *Rethinking Disability Policy*, Joseph Rowntree Foundation, 2011, jrf.org.uk/report/rethinking-disability-policy

Mullen, B, (ed) *Mad to be Normal: Conversations with R D Laing*, London, Free Association Books, 1995

McIntyre, A, "Breaking the Chains of Reason" in Blackledge, P and Davidson N (eds), *Alasdair MacIntyre's Engagement with Marxism*, Chicago, Haymarket Books, 2009

Neale, J, *The American War: Vietnam 1960-1975*, London, Bookmarks, 2001

Ollman, B, Alienation: *Marx's Conception of Man in Capitalist Society*, Cambridge, 1977

O'Hara, M, "Employers need to do more to overcome stigma at work", *Guardian*, 16 July 2013

Parry-Jones, H L, *The Trade in Lunacy: A Study of Private Madhouses in England in the Eighteenth and Nineteenth*

*Centuries*, London, Routledge, 1972/2007

Pick, D, *Psychoanalysis: a Very Short Introduction*, 2015, Oxford, Oxford University Press

Pilgrim, D, "Peter Sedgwick, Proto-critical realist?", *Critical and Radical Social Work*, 2016, vol 4, 3, p332

Porter, R, *Madness: a Short History*, Oxford: Oxford University Press, 2003

Read, J and Sanders, P, *The Causes of Mental Health Problems*, Ross-on-Wye, PCCCS Books, 2010

Read, J, "Childhood adversity and psychosis", in Read, J and Dillon, J (eds), *Models of Madness* (2nd ed), London, Routledge, 2013

Read, J, Bentall, R, Johnstone, L, Fosse, R and Bracken, P, "Electroconvulsive Therapy", in Read J and Dillon J (eds), *Models of Madness*, 2nd ed, London, Routledge, 2013

Read, J, Bentall, R P and Fosse, R, "Time to abandon the Bio-bio-bio model of psychosis; Exploring the Epigenetic and Psychological Mechanisms by which Adverse Life Events lead to Psychotic Symptoms" in Speed, E, Moncrieff, J and Rapley, M (eds), *De-Medicalizing Misery II*, Basingstoke, Palgrave Macmillan, 2014

Reid, J, Alienation, 1972, gla.ac.uk/media/media_167194_en.pdf

Recovery in the Bin, *20 Key Principles*, recoveryinthebin.org/recovery-in-the-bin-19-principless/

Rees, J, *The Algebra of Revolution*, London, Routledge, 1998

Rogers, A and Pilgrim, D, *Mental Health Policy in Britain: a Critical Introduction*, Basingstoke, Palgrave Macmillan, 1996

Rose, H and Rose, S, *Can Neuroscience Change Our Minds?*, London, Polity, 2016

Rose, N, *Our Psychiatric Future: the Politics of Mental Health, Cambridge,* Polity Press, 2019

Rosenhan, D, "On being sane in insane places", *Science*, 1972179 (4070), pp250-258

Rosenthal, S, "What's wrong with Sigmund Freud?", *Socialist Review*, 414, July/August, 2015

Royle, C, "Marxism and the Anthropocene", *International Socialism* 151, 2016, isj.org.uk/marxism-and-the-anthropocene/

Sample, I, "Covid poses 'greatest threat to mental health since Second World War,'" *Guardian*, 27 December 2020, www.theguardian.com/society/2020/dec/27/covid-poses-greatest-threat-to-mental-health-since-second-world-war

Sapey, B, Spandler, H and Anderson, J (eds), *Madness, Distress and the Politics of Disablement*, Bristol, Policy Press, 2015

Skopeliti, C and S Gecsoyler "'Terrified for my future': climate crisis takes heavy toll on young people's mental health", *Guardian*, 30 March 2023, www.theguardian.com/environment/2023/mar/30/terrified-for-my-future-climate-crisis-takes-heavy-toll-on-young-peoples-mental-health/

Scull, A, *Museums of Madness: the Social Organisation of Insanity in 19th Century England*, London, Allen Lane, 1979

Scull, A, *Madness in Civilisation*, London, Thames and Hudson, 2015

Scull, A, *Desperate Remedies: Psychiatry and the Mysteries of Mental Illness,* London, Allen Lane, 2022

Sedgwick, P, "Who's Mad—You or the System?", *Socialist Worker*, 5 February 1972

Sedgwick, P, *Psychopolitics*, Unkant Publishers, 1982/2015

Serge, V, "Life and Culture in 1918"in *From Lenin to Stalin*, New York, Pathfinder Press, 1973

Shah, P and Mountain, D, "The medical model is dead—long live the medical model", *The British Journal of Psychiatry*, 191, (5) 375-377, 2007

Shenker, J, *The Egyptians: a Radical Story*, Allen Lane, 2016

Shridar, D, "Was the pandemic bad for mental health? It depends who you ask", *Guardian*, 10 March 2023, www.theguardian.com/commentisfree/2023/mar/10/pandemic-mental-health-covid-lockdown

Smail, D, *Power, Interest and Psychology*, Ross-on-Wye, PCCS Books, 2005

SWAN Mental Health Charter, 2014, socialworkfuture.org/attachments/article/172/SWAN%20Mental%20Health%20Charter.pdf

Swain, D, *Alienation: an Introduction to Marx's Theory*, London, Bookmarks, 2012

Syall, R, "'Police in England and Wales dealing with more mental health crises than ever", *Guardian*, 23 February 2023, theguardian.com/uk-news/2023/feb/21/mental-health-crises-police-england-and-wales

Taylor, B, *The Last Asylum: A Memoir of Madness in our Times*, Hamish Hamilton, 2014

Tew, J, "Towards a socially situated model of mental distress", in Spandler, H, Anderson J and Sapey B (eds) *Madness, Distress and the Politics of Disablement*, Bristol, Policy Press, 2015, pp69-81

Time to Change (2014) time-to-change.org.uk/sites/default/files/121168_Attitudes_to_mental_illness_2013_report.pdf

Tooze, A, *Shutdown: How Covid Shook the World's Economy*, London, Allen Lane, 2021

Turkle, S, *Psychoanalytic Politics: Jacques Lacan and Freud's French Revolution*, 2nd edition, London, Free Association Books, 1992

Voloshinov, V N, *Freudianism: a Marxist Critique*, London, Verso, 1927/2012

Wallace, R, *Big Farms make Big Flu: Dispatches on Infectious Disease, Agribusiness and the Nature of Science*, New York, Monthly Review Press, 2016

Warner, R, *Recovery from Schizophrenia: Psychiatry and Political Economy*, 2nd ed, London, Routledge, 1994

Wastell, D and White , S, "Blinded by neuroscience: social policy, the family and the infant brain", *Families, Relationships and Society*, 2012, vol 1, issue 3: 397-414

WHO Europe, 2014, euro.who.int/en/health-topics/noncommunicable-diseases/mental-health/data-and-statistics

WHO, "Depression", 2016, who.int/mediacentre/factsheets/fs369/en/

Wilkinson, R and Pickett, K, *The Spirit Level: Why Equality is Better for Everyone*, London, Penguin, 2010

Zeilig, L, "Frantz Fanon's radical psychiatry: the making of a revolutionary", *Critical and Radical Social Work*, 2017, 5 (1), pp93-110

Žižek, S, *How to Read Lacan*, London, Granta, 2006

# Notes

**Notes for 2023 Introduction**

1    A Callinicos, *The New Age of Catastrophe*, Cambridge, Polity Press, 2023, pp7-8.

2    A Tooze, *Shutdown: How Covid Shook the World's Economy*, London, Allen Lane, 2021, p5.

3    I Sample, "Covid poses 'greatest threat to mental health since Second World War,'" *Guardian*, 27 December 2020, www.theguardian.com/society/2020/dec/27/covid-poses-greatest-threat-to-mental-health-since-second-world-war

4    WHO, "Mental Health and Covid-19: Early Evidence of the pandemic's impact", 2 March 2022, *WHO*, p6.

5    B Thombs and 25 others, "Comparison of mental health symptoms before and during the covid-19 pandemic: evidence from a systematic review and meta-analysis of 134 cohorts", *BMJ*.

6    D Shridar, "Was the pandemic bad for mental health? It depends who you ask", *Guardian*, 10 March 2023, www.theguardian.com/commentisfree/2023/mar/10/pandemic-mental-health-covid-lockdown

7    Oxfam International, "Ten richest men double their fortunes in pandemic while incomes of 99 percent of humanity fall", *Oxfam International,* 17 January, 2022

8    R Bentall, "Has the pandemic really caused a 'tsunami' of mental health problems?", *Guardian*, 9 February 2021, www.theguardian.com/commentisfree/2021/feb/09/pandemic-mental-health-problems-research-coronavirus

9    I Ferguson "Capitalism, Coronavirus and Mental Distress", *International Socialism* 168, autumn 2020, pp83-107, www.isj.org.uk/coronavirus-mental-distress/

10   M Smith, "Public overwhelmingly backs the government's new measures to tackle coronavirus", YouGov, 24 March 2020, www.yougov.co.uk/topics/health/articles-reports/2020/03/24/public-overwhelmingly-backs-governments-new-measures/

11   Shridar, 2023.

12   R Wallace, *Big Farms make Big Flu: Dispatches on Infectious Disease, Agribusiness and the Nature of Science,* New York, Monthly Review Press, 2016; M Davis, *The Monster Enters: Covid-19, the Avian Flu and the Plagues of Capitalism,* London, Verso, 2020.

13   E Lawrence, R Thompson, G Fontana and N Jennings, "The impact of climate change on mental health and emotional wellbeing: current evidence and implications for policy and practice", Imperial College London, May 2021, www.imperial.ac.uk/grantham/publications/all-publications/the-impact-of-climate-change-on-mental-health-and-emotional-wellbeing-current-evidence-and-implications-for-policy-and-practice.php; see also *WHO, Mental Health Policy Brief,* 3 June 2021.

14   "Mental health impact of climate change", *BACP*, 15 October 2020, www.bacp.co.uk/news/news-from-bacp/2020/15-october-mental-health-impact-of-climate-change/

15   C Skopeliti and S Gecsoyler "'Terrified for my future': climate crisis takes heavy toll on young people's mental health", *Guardian*, 30 March 2023, www.theguardian.com/environment/2023/

mar/30/terrified-for-my-future-climate-crisis-takes-heavy-toll-on-young-peoples-mental-health/

16   Skopeliti and Gecsoyler, 2023.

17   Examples include N Rose, *Our Psychiatric Future: the Politics of Mental Health, Cambridge,* Polity Press, 2019; N Filer, *The Heartland: Finding and Losing Schizophrenia,* London, Faber and Faber, 2019; A Scull, *Desperate Remedies: Psychiatry and the Mysteries of Mental Illness,* London, Allen Lane, 2022; J Davies, *Sedated: How Modern Capitalism Created Our Mental Health Crisis,* London, Atlantic Books, 2022, pp287-289.

18   J Moncrieff, R E Cooper, T Stockmann and others, "The serotonin theory of depression: a systematic umbrella review of the evidence", *Molecular Psychiatry,* 2022.

19   J Moncrieff, "The Political Economy of the Mental Health System: A Marxist Analysis," *Frontiers in Sociol*ogy, 2022.

20   L Johnstone and M Boyle, with J Cromby, J Dillon, D Harper, P Kinderman, E Longden, D Pilgrim and J Read, "The Power Threat Meaning Framework: Towards the identification of patterns in emotional distress, unusual experiences and troubled or troubling behaviour, as an alternative to functional psychiatric diagnosis", *British Psychological Society*, 2018.

21   M Boyle and L Johnstone, *A Straight Talking Introduction to the Power Threat Meaning Framework: an Alternative to Psychiatric Diagnosis,* London, PCCS Books, 2020.

22   L Johnstone, "Beyond the Mental Health Paradigm", *iai news*, 5 May 2021, www.iai.tv/articles/beyond-the-mental-health-paradigm-the-power-threat-meaning-framework-auid-1803

23   L Johnstone "Publication of the Power Threat Meaning Framework", *Mad in America*, 12 January 2018, www.madinamerica.com/2018/01/publication-power-threat-meaning-framework/

24   Davies, 2022.

25   D Campbell, "Millions with mental health needs not seeking NHS help, watchdog says", *Guardian*, 9 February 2023, www.theguardian.com/society/2023/feb/09/millions-with-mental-health-needs-not-seeking-nhs-help-watchdog-says/

26   R Hall "'Buckling' NHS fails to treat 250,000 children with mental health problems", *Guardian*, 16 April 2023, www.theguardian.com/education/2023/apr/16/buckling-nhs-fails-to-treat-250000-children-with-mental-health-problems/

27   R Booth, "Government 'to cut £250m from social care workforce funding' in England", *Guardian*, 17 March 2023, www.theguardian.com/society/2023/mar/17/government-to-cut-250m-from-social-care-workforce-funding-in-england-report-says/

28   R Syall, "'Police in England and Wales dealing with more mental health crises than ever", *Guardian*, 23 February 2023, www.theguardian.com/uk-news/2023/feb/21/mental-health-crises-police-england-and-wales

29   On the collapse of Corbynism see C Kimber, "Why did Labour Lose?", *International Socialism* 166, spring 2020, www.isj.org.uk/why-did-labour-lose/; On Scottish independence see B Fotheringham, D Sherry and C Bryce (eds) *Breaking Up the British State: Scotland, Independence and Socialism,* London, Bookmarks, 2021.

30   S Poggioli, "A public mental health model in Italy earns global praise. Now it faces its demise", *npr,* 24 November 2021; See also T Burns and J Foot, *Basaglia's International Legacy: From Asylums to Community,* Oxford University Press, 2020.

31   LJP de Aguiar, MIB Bellini and APV Ronsani, "Brazilian psychiatric reform: advances and constraints", *Critical and Radical Social Work*, March 2022, pp93-108.

32   Ferguson, 2020.

33   J Choonara, "The British Labour Movements Halting Recovery", *International Socialism* 178, spring 2023, www.isj.org.uk/halting-recovery/

34  D Conn, "Revealed: Tory peer Michelle Mone secretly received £29m from 'VIP lane' PPE firm", *Guardian*, 23 November, www.theguardian.com/uk-news/2022/nov/23/revealed-tory-peer-michelle-mone-secretly-received-29m-from-vip-lane-ppe-firm

35  Choonara, 2023.

36  K Marx and F Engels, *The German Ideology*, 1845, www.marxists.org/archive/marx/works/1845/german-ideology/cho1.htm#d4/

37  W Benjamin, *Selected Writings, Volume 4, 1938-40*, Harvard University Press, 2003, p392.

38  C Kimber, "'The strike is liberating'—day 11 of French revolt", *Socialist Worker*, 6 April 2023, www.socialistworker.co.uk/international/the-strike-is-liberating-day-11-of-french-revolt/

## Notes for 2017 Edition

1  B Sapey, H Spandler and J Anderson (eds), *Madness, Distress and the Politics of Disablement*, Bristol, Policy Press, 2015, p6.

2  C Wright Mills, *The Sociological Imagination*, USA, Oxford University Press, 1959/2000, pp8-11.

3  WHO, "Depression", 2016, www.who.int/mediacentre/factsheets/fs369/en/

4  WHO Europe, 2014, www.euro.who.int/en/health-topics/noncommunicable-diseases/mental-health/data-and-statistics.

5  Mental Health Foundation, *Fundamental Facts about Mental Health 2015*, mentalhealth.org.uk/publications/fundamental-facts-about-mental-health-2015.

6  Mental Health Foundation, *Surviving or Thriving? The State of the UK's Mental Health*, 2017.

7  M Knapp, "Mental health in an age of austerity", *Evidence-Based Mental Health Notebook*, 2012, ebmh.bmj.com/content/15/3/54.

8  J Henley, "Recessions can hurt but austerity kills", *Guardian*, 13 May 2013, www.theguardian.com/society/2013/may/15/recessions-hurt-but-austerity-kills.

9  Health and Safety Executive, 2016, hse.gov.uk/statistics/causdis/stress/.

10  T Adams, "Is there to much stress on stress?", *Guardian*, 14 February 2016, theguardian.com/society/2016/feb/14/workplace-stress-hans-selye.

11  C Harman, *Zombie Capitalism*, Bookmarks, 2009, p137.

12  W Davies, *The Happiness Industry*, Verso, 2013. See also I Ferguson, "Neoliberalism, happiness and well-being", *International Socialism*, 2007, isj.org.uk/neoliberalism-happiness-and-wellbeing/.

13  T Lott, "What does depression feel like? Trust me, you really don't want to know", *Guardian*, 19 April 2016, theguardian.com/commentisfree/2016/apr/19/depression-awareness-mental-illness-feel-like.

14  R D Laing, *Wisdom, Madness and Folly: The Making of a Psychiatrist*, Edinburgh, Canongate Classics, 2001, p9.

15  P Sedgwick, *Psychopolitics*, Unkant Publishers, 1982/2015, p41.

16  G Brown and T Harris, *Social Origins of Depression: a Study of Psychiatric Disorder in Women*, London, Tavistock Publications, 1978, p3.

17  I Deutscher, *The Prophet Outcast*, Oxford, Oxford University Press, 1970, pp150-151.

18  T Eagleton, *Materialism*, New Haven and London, Yale University Press, 2017.

19  H Devlin, "Living near heavy traffic increases risk of dementia, say scientists", *Guardian*, 5 January 2017, www.theguardian.com/society/2017/jan/04/living-near-heavy-traffic-increases-dementia-risk-say-scientists.

20  R Warner, *Recovery from Schizophrenia: Psychiatry and Political Economy*, 2nd ed, London, Routledge, 1994.

21  N Geras, *Marxism and Human Nature: Refutation of a Legend*, London, Verso, 1983/2016, pp72-73.

22  T Eagleton, *Why Marx was Right*, Yale University Press, 2011, pp137-138.

23  E Durkheim, *Suicide: a Study in Sociology*, snowballpublishing.com, 2013.

24  J Read and P Sanders, *The Causes of Mental Health Problems*, Ross-on-Wye, PCCCS Books, 2010, p124.

25  Mental Health Foundation, *Fundamental Facts about Mental Health*, London, Mental Health Foundation, 2016.

26  R Wilkinson and K Pickett, *The Spirit Level: Why Equality is Better for Everyone*, London, Penguin, 2010.

27  J Rees, *The Algebra of Revolution*, London, Routledge, 1998, pp7-8.

28  Brown and Harris, 1978, p275.

29  Health and Social Care Information Centre, BBC, 3 August 2013.

30  J Harris and V White, *Oxford Dictionary of Social Work and Social Care*, Oxford University Press, 2013.

31  A Scull, *Madness in Civilisation*, London, Thames and Hudson, 2015, p176.

32  Scull, p28.

33  Scull, pp27-28.

34  Scull, p105.

35  Scull, p101.

36  E Fee and T M Brown, "Freeing the Insane", *American Journal of Public Health*, October 2006, 96(10), p1743.

37  Scull, pp127-128.

38  H L Parry-Jones, *The Trade in Lunacy: A Study of Private Madhouses in England in the 18th and 19th Centuries*, London, Routledge, 1972/2007.

39  A Rogers and D Pilgrim, *Mental Health Policy in Britain: a Critical Introduction*, Basingstoke, Palgrave Macmillan, 1996, p50.

40  Taylor, B, *The Last Asylum: A Memoir of Madness in our Times*, Hamish Hamilton, 2014, pp102-103.

41  Taylor, p110.

42  M Foucault, *Madness and Civilization: A History of Insanity in the Age of Reason*, London, Routledge, 2001.

43  L Appignanesi, *Mad, Bad and Sad: A History of Women and the Mind Doctors from 1800 to the Present*, London, Virago, 2008, p105.

44  A Scull, *Museums of Madness: the Social Organisation of Insanity in 19th Century England*, London, Allen Lane, 1979, p35.

45  F Engels, *The Condition of the Working-Class in England*, London, Lawrence and Wishart, 1844/1973, p122.

46  Cited in Scull, p229.

47  Sedgwick, p148.

48  Scull, Chapter 10, gives a good, albeit horrific, account of these treatments.

49  Scull, p298.

50  T Burns, *Our Necessary Shadow: The Nature and Meaning of Psychiatry*, London, Allen Lane Burns, 2013, p201.

51  Burns, pp202-203.

52  Lorenz, W, *Social Work in a Changing Europe*, London, Routledge, 1994, pp34-35.

53  Sedgwick, p218.

54  Hunter and McAlpine, cited in R Porter, *Madness: a Short History*, Oxford, Oxford University Press, 2003, pp156-157 (my emphasis).

55  Cited in Porter, p160.

56  Scull, p308.

57  Porter, p205.

58  Scull, p369.

59  King's Fund, *Mental Health Under Pressure*, 2015.

60  Sedgwick, pp193-194.

61  Scull, p375.

62  D Rosenhan, "On being sane in insane places", *Science*, vol 179, January 1973, pp250-258, web.cocc.edu/lminorevans/on_being_sane_in_insane_places.htm.

63  G Greenberg, *The Book of Woe: the DSM and the Unmaking of Psychiatry*, Scribe UK, 2013, p20.

64  Greenberg, p36.

65  Greenberg, p 41.

66  J Davies, *Cracked: Why Psychiatry is Doing More Harm Than Good*, Iconbooks, 2014, pp160-161.

67  J Davies, p53.

68  J Davies, pp53-54.

69  Cited in J Davies, p55.

70  R Bentall, *Doctoring the Mind: Why Psychiatric Treatments Fail*, Penguin, 2010, pp144-145.

71  P Bracken, P Thomas, S Timimi et al, "Psychiatry beyond the current paradigm", *British Journal of Psychiatry*,

2012, 201, pp430-434.

72  Bentall, 2010, p198.

73  Bentall, 2010, p197.

74  Scull, quoted in Burns, p xii.

75  Burns, p xv.

76  Burns, p xvii.

77  P Shah and D Mountain "The medical model is dead—long live the medical model", *The British Journal of Psychiatry*, 2007, 191 (5) 375-377, p375.

78  J Read, R Bentall, L Johnstone, R Fosse and P Bracken, "Electroconvulsive Therapy", in J Read and J Dillon (eds) *Models of Madness*, 2nd ed, London, Routledge, 2013, pp90-104, p101.

79  N Davis and P Duncan "Electroconvulsive therapy on the rise again in England", *Guardian*, 17 April 2017.

80  Otto Fenichel, cited in R Jacoby, *The Repression of Psychoanalysis: Otto Fenichel and the Political Freudians*, Chicago, University of Chicago Press, 1983, p120.

81  D Herzog, *Cold War Freud: Psychoanalysis in an Age of Catastrophes*, Cambridge, Cambridge University Press, 2017, p84.

82  Cited in Appignanesi, p419.

83  L Miles, "Transgender oppression and resistance", *International Socialism* 141, 2014, pp37-70, pp58-59.

84  S Frosh, *A Brief Introduction to Psychoanalytic Theory*, Basingstoke, Palgrave Macmillan, 2012, p5.

85  S Blumenthal, "A Short History of the Trump Family, *London Review of Books*, vol 39, no 4, 16 February 2017, pp32-37.

86  D Smail, *Power, Interest and Psychology*, Ross-on-Wye, PCCS Books, 2005, pp2-3.

87  Quoted in I Deutscher, *The Prophet Unarmed*, Oxford, Oxford University Press, 1970, p180.

88  A McIntyre, "Breaking the Chains of Reason" in P Blackledge and N Davidson (eds), *Alasdair MacIntyre's Engagement with Marxism*, Chicago, Haymarket Books, 2009, p160.

89  Jacoby, p39.

90  J Lear, *Freud*, 2nd ed, London, Routledge, 2015, p13.

91  S Freud, "The Question of a

Weltanschauung" in P Gay (ed), *The Freud Reader*, London, Vintage Books, 1995, p798.

92  Frosh, p11.

93  Cited in Lear, p29.

94  J Kovel, *A Complete Guide to Therapy: From Psychoanalysis to Behaviour Modification*, Harmondsworth, Penguin, 1978, p116.

95  Herzog.

96  S Rosenthal, "What's wrong with Sigmund Freud?", *Socialist Review*, 414, July/August 2015.

97  S Freud, "An Autobiographical Study, in Gay, p20.

98  V N Voloshinov, *Freudianism: a Marxist Critique*, London: Verso, 1927/2012, p9.

99  S Freud in Gay, p20.

100 J Masson, *The Assault on Truth: Freud's Suppression of the Seduction Theory*, Pocket Books, 1998.

101 Lear, pp73-74.

102 Lear, p74.

103 Frosh, p18.

104 J Mitchell, *Psychoanalysis and Feminism*, London, Penguin, 1974.

105 Lear, pp76-78.

106 Marx, K, *Capital*, vol 1, London, Penguin, 1976, p284.

107 Freud, 1905.

108 Appignanesi, p423.

109 Herzog, p84.

110 V Serge, "Life and Culture in 1918"in *From Lenin to Stalin*, New York, Pathfinder Press, 1973, p119.

111 Miller, M, *Freud and the Bolsheviks*, New Haven and London: Yale University Press, 1998, p70.

112 Cited in M Miller, *Freud and the Bolsheviks*, New Haven and London, Yale University Press, 1998, p57.

113 Miller, p68.

114 A Collier, "Lacan, psychoanalysis and the Left", *International Socialism* 7 (Winter 1989), pp51- 71.

115 Jacoby, p12.

116 Jacoby, p12.

117 Kovel, p178.

118 Herzog.

119 S Turkle, *Psychoanalytic Politics: Jacques Lacan and Freud's French Revolution*, 2nd edition, London, Free Association

Books, 1992.

120 John Molyneux, "What is the Real Marxist Tradition?", *International Socialism*, July 1983, marxists.org/history/etol/writers/molyneux/1983/07/tradition.htm.

121 Quoted in C Harman, 1988, p94.

122 Turkle, pp9-10.

123 Turkle, p10.

124 D Pick, *Psychoanalysis: a Very Short Introduction*, Oxford, Oxford University Press, 2015, p87.

125 T Eagleton, 2017, p86.

126 Frosh, p180.

127 Frosh, p181.

128 Eagleton, *Trouble with Strangers: a Study of Ethics*, Chichester, Wiley-Blackwell 2009, p83.

129 S Žižek, *How to Read Lacan*, 2006, London: Granta, p65.

130 Frosh, p181.

131 Eagleton, 2009, p142-143.

132 A Collier, "Lacan, psychoanalysis and the left", *International Socialism* 7, 1980, p67.

133 Collier, p68.

134 A Callinicos, *Social Theory: a Historical Introduction*, London, Polity, 1999, pp190-191.

135 Herzog, p17.

136 J N Clarke cited in B M Z Cohen, *Psychiatric Hegemony: a Marxist Theory of Mental Illness*, Palgrave Macmillan, 2017.

137 D Forgacs (ed), *The Antonio Gramsci Reader*, London, Lawrence and Wishart, 1999, pp333-334. For an excellent discussion of Gramsci's ideas, see C Harman, "Gramsci, the Prison Notebooks and philosophy", *International Socialism* 114, 2007, isj.org.uk/gramsci-the-prison-notebooks-and-philosophy/

138 I Ferguson, "Between Marx and Freud: Erich Fromm Revisited", *International Socialism* 149, 2016, pp151-174.

139 D Cooper (ed), *The Dialectics of Liberation*, London, Verso, 1968/2015.

140 Sedgwick, *Psychopolitics*, 1982/2015, Unkant Publishers, p66

141 Cited in Rogers and Pilgrim, p70.

142 B Mullen (ed), *Mad to be Normal:*

*Conversations with R D Laing*, London, Free Association Books, 1995, p261.

143 R D Laing, *The Divided Self*, London, Pelican, 1960/1965, pp30-31.

144 Sedgwick, p74.

145 Sedgwick, pp75-76.

146 Sedgwick, p76-77.

147 Laing (1960/1965), p11.

148 R D Laing and A Esterson, *Sanity, Madness and the Family*, 2nd ed, London, Pelican, 1969, p12.

149 R D Laing, *The Politics of Experience*, London, Pelican, 1967, p100.

150 Laing, 1967, p101.

151 Laing, 1967, p101.

152 Laing, 1967, p106.

153 Mitchell, p279.

154 Mitchell, pp291-292.

155 Sedgwick, p30, p32 (emphasis in original).

156 Sedgwick, p25.

157 Sedgwick, p33.

158 Sedgwick, p38.

159 Sedgwick, p38.

160 Sedgwick, p39.

161 Sedgwick, pp40-41.

162 Sedgwick, p99.

163 Sedgwick, p99-100.

164 Sedgwick, p100.

165 Laing, 1967, p95 (emphasis in original).

166 P Beresford, "From psycho-politics to mad studies: learning from the legacy of Peter Sedgwick", *Critical and Radical Social Work*, 4 (3), 2016, pp343-355.

167 D Pilgrim, "Peter Sedgwick, proto-critical realist?", *Critical and Radical Social Work*, 4 (3), 2016, pp327-341.

168 Brown and Harris, 1978, p275.

169 Z Kotowicz, *R D Laing and the Paths of Anti-Psychiatry*, London, Routledge, 1997, p96.

170 Kotowicz, p98.

171 P Sedgwick, "Who's Mad—You or the System?", *Socialist Worker*, 5 February 1972.

172 Kotowicz, p97.

173 G Brown, J Birley and J Wing, "Influence of family life on the course of schizophrenic disorder: a replication", *British Journal of Psychiatry*, 121, 1972, pp241-258.

174 Laing, 1967, p96 (my emphasis).
175 D Pilgrim, "Peter Sedgwick, Proto-critical realist?", *Critical and Radical Social Work*, vol 4, 3, 2016, p332.
176 SWAN Mental Health Charter, 2014, socialworkfuture.org/attachments/article/172/SWAN%20Mental%20Health%20Charter.pdf.
177 J Foot, *The Man who Closed the Asylums: Franco Basaglia and the Revolution in Mental Health Care*, London, Verso, 2015.
178 L Zeilig, "Frantz Fanon's radical psychiatry: the making of a revolutionary", *Critical and Radical Social Work*, 5 (1), 2017, pp93-110.
179 Foot.
180 J Dillon, L Johnstone and E Longden, "Trauma, Dissociation, Attachment and Neuroscience: a New Paradigm for Understanding Severe Mental Distress" in E Speed, J Moncrieff and M Rapley (eds), *De-medicalizing Misery II*, 2014, p226.
181 J Tew, "Towards a socially situated model of mental distress", in H Spandler, J Anderson and B Sapey (eds) *Madness, Distress and the Politics of Disablement*, 2015, Bristol, Policy Press, p80.
182 N Hollander, *Love in a Time of Hate: Liberation Psychology in Latin America*, New Jersey, Brunswick Press, 1997, p110.
183 R Bentall, "Mental illness is the result of misery, yet still we stigmatise it", *Guardian*, 26 February 2016, theguardian.com/commentisfree/2016/feb/26/mental-illness-misery-childhood-traumas. See also R Bentall, *Madness Explained: Psychosis and Human Nature*, London, Penguin, 2003, pp477-483.
184 Cited in J Read, "Childhood adversity and psychosis", in J Read and J Dillon (eds), *Models of Madness* (2nd ed), London, Routledge, 2013, p249.
185 Read, 2013, p263.
186 I Ferguson, M Petrie and K Stalker, *Developing Accessible Services for Homeless People with Severe Mental Distress and Behavioural Difficulties*, University of Stirling, 2005, p21.

187 J Read, R P Bentall and R Fosse, "Time to abandon the Bio-bio-bio model of psychosis; Exploring the Epigenetic and Psychological Mechanisms by which Adverse Life Events lead to Psychotic Symptoms" in E Speed, J Moncrieff and M Rapley (eds) *De-Medicalizing Misery II*, Basingstoke, Palgrave Macmillan, 2014, pp210-225.
188 Read and Sanders, pp36-37.
189 Bentall, 2016.
190 B van der Kolk, *The Body Keeps the Score: Mind, Body and Brain in the Transformation of Trauma*, London, Penguin, 2014, p66-67.
191 Van der Kolk, p67.
192 Dillon et al, p228.
193 Dillon et al, p232.
194 J Neale, *The American War: Vietnam 1960-1975*, London, Bookmarks, 2001, p186.
195 Hollander, pp110-111.
196 H Rose and S Rose, *Can Neuroscience Change Our Minds?*, London, Polity, 2016.
197 Rose and Rose, pp60-61.
198 G Allen, *Early Intervention: Smart Investment, Massive Savings, Independent Report*, HM Government, 2011.
199 Allen, 2011, p xiii.
200 Allen, 2011, p15.
201 Cited in D Wastell and S White, "Blinded by neuroscience: social policy, the family and the infant brain", *Families, Relationships and Society*, vol 1, issue 3: 397-414.
202 Rose and Rose, pp77-78.
203 Rose and Rose, pp82-83.
204 Cited in Wastell and White.
205 Rose and Rose, p87.
206 Taylor, p250.
207 I Ferguson, "Identity politics or class struggle? The case of the mental health users' movement" in M Lavalette and G Mooney (eds), *Class Struggle and Social Welfare*, London, Routledge, 2000, p235.
208 M O'Hara, "Employers need to do more to overcome stigma at work", *Guardian*, 16 July 2013.
209 Cited in I Ferguson, "Identity politics

or class struggle? The case of the mental health users' movement" in M Lavalette and G Mooney (eds), *Class Struggle and Social Welfare*, 2000, London, Routledge, p244.

210 Ferguson, 2000, p243.

211 P Campbell, "The history of the user movement in the United Kingdom" in T Heller, J Reynolds, R Gomm, R Musten and T Pattison (eds), *Mental Health Matters*, Basingstoke, Macmillan, 1996, pp218-225.

212 F Branfield and P Beresford, *Making User Involvement Work: Supporting Service User Networking and Knowledge*, York, Joseph Rowntree Foundation, 2006.

213 norfolksuffolkmentalhealth crisis.org. uk

214 bbc.co.uk/news/uk-england-cambridgeshire-26453052

215 R Menzies, B A LeFrancois and G Reaume, "Introducing Mad Studies" in B A LeFrancois, R Menzies and G Reaume (eds), *Mad Matters: a Critical Reader in Canadian Mad Studies*, Toronto, Canadian Scholars Press, 2013.

216 M Cresswell and H Spandler, "Solidarities and tensions in mental health politics: Mad Studies and Psychopolitics", *Critical and Radical Social Work*, 4: 3, 2016, pp357-373, p360.

217 Cited in Cressell and Spandler, pp359-360.

218 Cohen, pp207-208.

219 S Moore, "The lesson of Prince Harry's grief? We need mental health services for all", *Guardian*, 17 April 2017.

220 Callinicos, p192.

221 Eagleton, 2016, p86.

222 K Marx, *Theses on Feuerbach*, marxists. org/archive/marx/works/1845/theses/theses.htm.

223 Marx, Capital, p759.

224 K Marx and F Engels, *The German Ideology*, 1846, marxists.org/archive/marx/works/1845/german-ideology/cho1a.htm.

225 C Royle, "Marxism and the Anthropocene", *International*

226 Eagleton, 2011, p81.

227 Marx, *Capital*, pp283-284.

228 Rees, p90.

229 Cited in P Blackledge, *Marxism and Ethics*, State University of New York Press, 2012, p56.

230 Rees, p89.

231 C Harman, *Zombie Capitalism*, Bookmarks, 2009, p37.

232 B Ollman, *Alienation: Marx's Conception of Man in Capitalist Society*, Cambridge, 1977, p131.

233 This section draws extensively on I Ferguson and M Lavalette "Beyond Power Discourse: Alienation and Social Work", *British Journal of Social Work*, 2004.

234 K Marx, "Economic and Philosophical Manuscripts" in K Marx, *Early Writings*, Harmondsworth, Penguin, 1844/1975, p326.

235 Ollman, p206.

236 Wilkinson and Pickett, p75.

237 D Swain, *Alienation: an Introduction to Marx's Theory*, Bookmarks, 2012, p66.

238 J Reid, *Alienation*, 1972, gla.ac.uk/media/media_167194_en.pdf.

239 N Davies, *Dark Heart*, London, Vintage, 1998, p110.

240 Davies, 1998, p82.

241 Burns, 2013, p xiii

242 Quoted in I Ferguson, "The Potential and Limits of Mental Health Service User Involvement", PhD Thesis, University of Glasgow, 1999, p173.

243 P Kinderman, "A Manifesto for Psychological Health and Wellbeing" in J Davies (ed), *The Sedated Society: The Causes and Harms of our Psychiatric Drug Epidemic*, Basingstoke, Palgrave Macmillan, pp291-292.

244 J Morris, *Rethinking Disability Policy*, Joseph Rowntree Foundation, 2011, jrf. org.uk/report/rethinking-disability-policy.

245 scottishrecovery.net

246 P Deegan, "Recovery and the Conspiracy of Hope", Conference presentation, 1996, patdeegan.com/pat-deegan/lectures/conspiracy-of-hope.

247 Recovery in the Bin, *20 Key Principles*, recoveryinthebin.org/recovery-in-the-bin-19-principless/

248 Independent Living in Scotland, ilis.co.uk/independent-living.

249 Taylor, p264.

250 D Campbell, "Prescription of anti-depressants at all time high", *Guardian*, 29 June 2017, theguardian.com/society/2017/jun/29/nhs-prescribed-record-number-of-antidepressants-last-year.

251 Brown and Harris, p3.

252 K Marx, Capital, pp375-376.

253 Time to Change, *Attitudes to Mental Illness 2013 Research Report*, 2014 time-to-change.org.uk/sites/default/files/121168_Attitudes_to_mental_illness_2013_report.pdf.

254 C Barker and K Weber, "Solidarnosc: from Gdansk to Military Repression", *International Socialism* 15, 1982, p148.

255 J Shenker, *The Egyptians: a Radical Story*, Allen Lane, 2016, p12.

# Index